Julie Hasler's
Cross Stitch
Designs

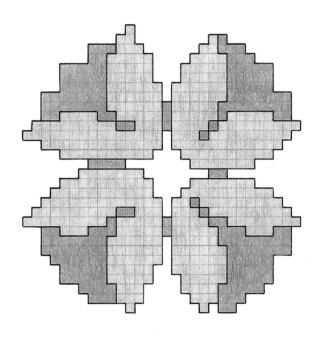

Julie Hasler's
Cross Stitch
Designs

St. Martin's Griffin
New York

ACKNOWLEDGMENTS

The author would like to thank the following people for their invaluable help in creating this book – Lesley Smith for design ideas, and the following ladies for the lovely embroideries: Stella Baddeley, Lesley Buckerfield, Odette Harrison, Maureen Hipgrave and Lynda Potter.

Library of Congress Cataloging-in-Publication Data
Hasler, Julie S.
    Julie Hasler's cross stitch designs / Julie Hasler.
        p.   cm.
    ISBN 0–312–13419–3
    1. Cross-stitch—Patterns.   I. Title.
TT778.C76H37335   1995
746.44′3041—dc20   95–13979
                                                CIP

First St. Martin's Griffin Edition: 1995

10 9 8 7 6 5 4 3 2 1

First published in the United Kingdom in 1994 by
B.T. Batsford Ltd., 4 Fitzhardinge Street, London W1H 0AH

Typeset by J&L Composition Ltd.,
Station Avenue, Filey, North Yorkshire
Printed in Hong Kong

Contents

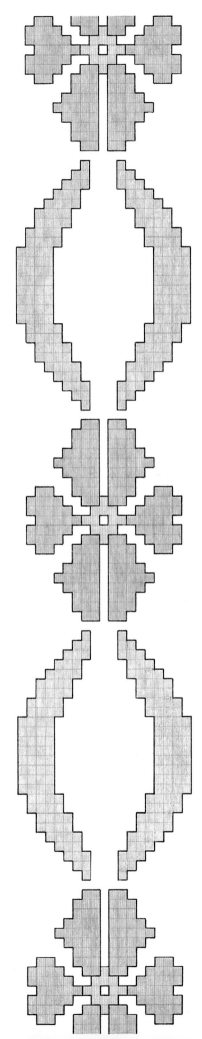

Introduction

Cross stitch has been a popular form of embroidery throughout the centuries, and in many different countries and cultures. In Tudor and Elizabethan England people used fine cross stitch to decorate shirts and chemises. Victorian ladies of leisure worked cross stitch designs in heavy Berlin wool-work; these were mostly used on decorative household items such as cushions, rugs, footstools and firescreens. For many centuries, small girls learned their alphabets and numbers whilst they learned to sew, making beautiful samplers. Being so simple and versatile, cross stitch has adapted perfectly to the requirements of the needlewomen of every period.

The latest cross stitch revival burst upon us just a few years ago and has gone from strength to strength. Cross stitch is increasingly popular for the decoration of modern household furnishings, household linen and children's clothes. In fact, almost anything can lend itself to this type of embroidery.

Cross stitch is a very rewarding and inexpensive hobby. It is also very easy to learn. With a little practice, you will be able to achieve results that even an experienced needlewoman would be proud of. Whether you are an experienced or inexperienced needleworker, you will be able to find designs in this book to suit your abilities.

You do not have to follow the charts exactly if you do not wish to. The book explains how to create your own original designs by using different colours, or by combining different borders and motifs.

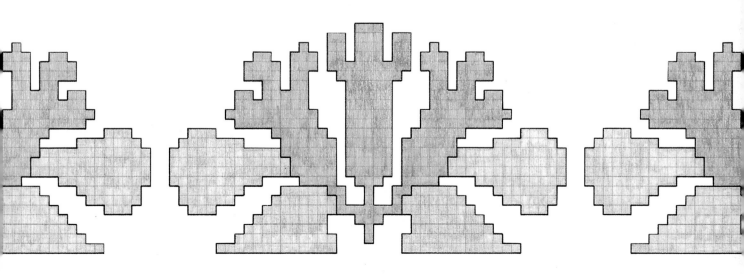

Creating your own designs

The designs in this book are divided into seven sections: Flowers, Animals, Birds, Historical Designs, Traditional Samplers, Geometric Designs, and Alphabets and Numerals. The designs are intended to be used as a starting-point, to which you can add your own details or colour choices, thereby creating your own unique design. The possibilities are endless. Some pages have been designed so that they can be stitched as complete pictures straight from the book.

Each section is preceded by a photograph of a finished embroidery, showing either a different colourway to the charts or a mixture of borders and motifs cleverly placed together to achieve different effects. Say, for example, you like the Mandarin Duck from page 48 but you think it would look good with a floral, or even a geometric, border. Simply find the border you like and put it together with the Mandarin Duck design. It is so easy!

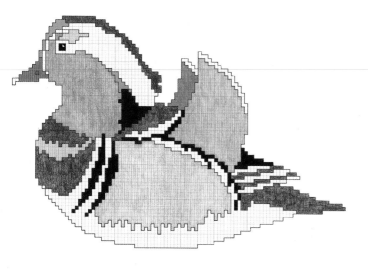

DESIGN EQUIPMENT

GRAPH PAPER

You will need good quality graph paper on which to draw your designs. There are many different grid sizes available from art shops and stationers; I find the best sizes are (metric) 2, 10 and 20 millimetres (imperial ¹⁄₁₀th inch, ½ inch and 1 inch). These technical sizes will be shown on the pad; what they actually mean is that the metric paper has 10 squares per 2 centimetres, and the imperial paper has 10 squares per 1 inch (2.5 cm).

You will need a piece of graph paper large enough for your final design, which means you may have to stick two pieces together (taking care that the grid lines match up). You will also need spare pieces of graph paper on which to draw the 'components' of your design.

For example, if you decide to design a picture for a Mother's Day gift, you might choose a large floral motif as the main feature of the design and lettering from one of the alphabets to write a message (or her name) underneath. You could complete your picture with a traditional sampler-style border to go all round the design. It is entirely up to you.

LEAD PENCIL

Find a pencil which you feel comfortable using. It should have quite a soft lead. I find either B or HB the best; if you get too soft a lead, it will smudge. If you do make a mistake, B or HB will erase easily without smudging. I use a good quality propelling pencil with a very fine lead.

COLOURED PENCILS

When you have drawn up the designs you want from the relevant pages and positioned them on your final design sheet, colour the charts in with the approximate colours that you intend to stitch your embroidery in. That way, you will get a good indication of what the final design will look like.

You can buy some wonderful coloured pencils from art shops. The Castell Polychromos range by

A. W. Faber and the Derwent Studio range by Rexel Cumberland both contain a wide colour range, but if you just want to buy a few cheap pencils a packet of children's crayons will suffice. More subtle shading will be achieved when you actually come to choosing your threads.

PENCIL SHARPENER

Both your pencils and coloured crayons need to be kept sharp. A blunt pencil will make inaccurate lines on the graph paper, and the patterns need to be copied correctly and accurately. You may find a scalpel or craft knife more useful, especially for the coloured pencils which often break in pencil sharpeners.

ERASER

It is certainly worth buying a good-quality eraser, such as a Pelikan or Staedtler. This will erase coloured pencil marks without smudging, as well as lead pencil marks. Art shops stock these erasers.

SCISSORS

A pair of paper-cutting scissors is used to cut out the various designs that you have drawn on graph paper, so that you can arrange them on your final design sheet. Do not use embroidery scissors or dressmaking scissors, as you will soon blunt them.

ADHESIVE

You will need adhesive to stick the sheets of graph paper together, and also to stick your various designs to the final design sheet once you have decided on their final position. Choose a glue which does not wet or distort the paper, and will also allow for repositioning if you make a mistake or change your mind. Adhesive is available in aerosol form from art shops (Photo Mount or Spray Mount by Scotch 3M are among the best adhesives for this type of work). Alternatively, you can use a solid glue in stick form.

MIRROR

When it comes to turning corners on borders, a small handbag mirror is essential. In some cases, it is obvious how and where to turn a straight border design at a right angle in order to make a corner, but with more complex designs you need to use a mirror. Place it diagonally across the design at 45° and move it along until a pleasing effect is reflected in the mirror. Copy down what you see in the reflection onto graph paper.

PUTTING A DESIGN TOGETHER

THE FINAL DESIGN SHEET

Stick sheets of graph paper together until you have a piece large enough to accommodate your final design. Measure it *exactly* both horizontally and vertically, divide by two and, with a faint pencil line, draw in the centre lines. This will help you to centralize the components of your design.

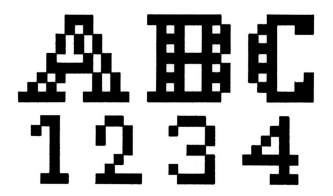

USING ALPHABETS AND NUMERALS

Decide on the alphabet you are going to use, then draw the lettering, names, numerals, etc. that you need on long strips of graph paper, which can be cut to size later to fit your design. If you make a mistake in the spacing between the words, do not worry as this can be rectified by cutting the paper and re-sticking it on your final design sheet. To centre a strip of lettering, simply count the number of squares it covers, divide by two and make a small mark at the centre point. Align this with the centre lines on your final design sheet.

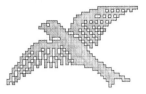

USING BORDERS

Choose a border and draw it on four long strips of graph paper to the approximate size you need. To enlarge a border, simply add more pattern repeats. Corners for use with continuous borders can be found in a number of the designs in this book. Non-continuous borders can also be created by placing a motif in each corner. The border may also benefit from an inner and outer retaining line, as featured in the Black Cat and Stag design on page 37.

SELECTING MOTIFS

When you have decided what you are going to make, look carefully through the choice of ideas in this book and think how you want your final design to look. For example, you may want to stitch a sampler incorporating animals and birds, or you may decide to leave an alphabet out of a sampler design, replacing it instead with a floral motif. Decide which motifs you want to use, and draw these on the graph paper.

CUTTING OUT YOUR DESIGN

Cut out the individual components of your design (motifs, lettering, borders, etc.), leaving a minimum of one clear square of graph paper around each. In the case of the motifs, cut them out as square or rectangular shapes. Put the cut-out pieces of graph paper in an envelope or clear plastic to keep them safe and clean.

HOW TO ARRANGE THE FINAL DESIGN

If you are using a border to surround your design, place the four border strips roughly in position on your final design sheet. Then place the other components of your design (lettering, motifs, etc.) inside the border. Move them around until a pleasing effect is achieved.

This method gives you time to change your mind and to try several different layouts if your original idea does not work. If a particular design or motif

does not fit, or looks out of place, it may be best to discard it and replace it with a different one.

Place the border strips in their final positions and adjust them if necessary. When you are satisfied with the design, fix all the components to the final design sheet with adhesive, ensuring that the grid lines (the squares) are in alignment with the grid lines on the design sheet. Finally, choose your colour scheme and colour in your design. Do not worry if you are not entirely happy with the effect when the whole design is coloured in. You can select different colours for certain parts of the design when you choose your embroidery threads.

How to do cross stitch

MATERIALS AND EQUIPMENT

NEEDLE

You will need a small, blunt tapestry needle, no 24 or no 26.

FABRIC

Evenweave fabrics on which it is easy to count the threads, such as Aida, Hardanger or Linda, are used for cross stitch. These fabrics are available in a wide choice of colours: white, ecru, black, red, blue, green and yellow, to name but a few. They come in varying thread counts, which give a range of stitches per inch, for example, 8, 11, 14, 16 and 18-count Aida, 22-count Hardanger and 27-count Linda. Do not use a fabric which does not have an even weave, as it will distort the embroidery.

THREADS

The designs in this book have been created for DMC six-stranded embroidery cottons, but a conversion chart is included on pages 17–19. The number of strands used will depend on the fabric you choose. For example, three strands for 11-count fabric, two strands for 14, 16 and 18-count fabric and one strand for 22-count and finer work.

EMBROIDERY HOOP

A 10, 12.5 or 15–centimetre (4, 5 or 6–inch) round plastic or wooden hoop with a screw-type tension adjuster is ideal for cross stitch.

SCISSORS

A pair of sharp embroidery scissors is essential, especially if a mistake has to be cut out. You will also need a large pair of scissors (ideally dressmaker's cutting-out scissors) to cut the fabric.

PREPARATION

To prevent the edges of the fabric from unravelling, you can cover them with a fold of masking tape or, alternatively, use whip-stitching or machine stitching.

Where you make your first stitch is important as it will position the finished design on the fabric. To begin with, you need to find the exact centre point of the chart. Count the squares (i.e. stitches) on the chart both vertically and horizontally. Divide each figure in half and mark the crossing point. Alternatively, measure both ways with a ruler and divide each measurement by two. Next locate the centre of the fabric by folding it in half vertically and then horizontally, pinching along the folds. Mark along these lines with basting stitches. The centre stitch of your design will be where the folds in the fabric cross.

It is best to begin stitching at the top of the design. To locate the top, count the squares up from the centre of the chart, then count left or right to the first symbol. Next count the corresponding number of holes up and across from the centre of the fabric, and begin stitching at that point. Each square on the chart represents a square on the fabric, and each colour represents the appropriate coloured stitch.

To insert the fabric in the embroidery hoop, place the area of fabric to be embroidered over the inner ring then gently push the outer ring over it. Gently and evenly pull the fabric, ensuring that it is drum-taut in the hoop and that the mesh is straight, tightening the screw adjuster as you go. When you are working, you will find it easier to have the screw in the '10 o'clock' position, to prevent the thread from becoming tangled in the screw with each stitch. If you are left-handed, have the screw in the '1 o'clock' position. You will find it necessary to re-tighten the fabric continually to keep it taut. Tension makes stitching easier, enabling you to push the

needle through the holes of the fabric without piercing the fibres.

When you are working with stranded cotton, always separate the strands and place them together again before threading your needle and beginning to stitch. Never double the thread; if you need to use two strands, use two separate strands. These simple rules will result in much better coverage of the fabric.

STITCH TECHNIQUES

CROSS STITCH

To begin a stitch, bring the needle up from the wrong side through a hole in the fabric (Fig. 1) at the left end of a row of stitches of the same colour. Fasten the thread by holding a short length of thread on the underside of the fabric and securing it with the first two or three stitches (Fig. 2). Never use a knot to fasten the thread as this will create a bumpy back surface, and the finished piece of work will not lie flat.

Next bring the needle across one square (or block) to the right, and one square above on a left-to-right diagonal. Insert the needle as in Fig. 1. Half of the cross stitch is now completed. Continue in this way until you reach the end of the row of stitches. Your stitches should be diagonal on the right side of the fabric and vertical on the wrong side.

To complete the upper half of the stitch, cross back from right to left to form an 'X' (Fig. 3). Work all the stitches in the row (Fig. 4).

Cross stitch can also be worked by crossing each stitch as you come to it, as you would do for isolated stitches. This method works just as well, and it is really a question of personal preference.

Work vertical rows of stitches as shown in Fig. 5. Finish all the threads by running your needle under four or more stitches on the wrong side of the work (Fig. 6). Cut the thread close.

When you are stitching, it is important not to pull the fabric out of shape. Work the stitches in two motions, straight up through a hole in the fabric and then straight down, making sure that the fabric remains taut. Do not pull the thread tight – snug, but not tight. If you follow this method, you will find that the thread lies just where you want it to and does not pull the fabric out of shape.

If the thread becomes twisted, drop the needle and let it hang down freely. It will then untwist itself. Do not continue working with twisted thread as it will look thinner and will not cover the fabric as well.

Never leave the needle in the design area of your work when not in use. No matter how good the needle, it could rust and might mark your work permanently.

Do not carry thread across an open expanse of fabric. If you are working separate areas of the same colour, finish off and begin again. Loose threads, especially dark colours, will be visible from the right side of your work when the project is completed.

BACKSTITCH

Backstitch is used in some of the designs, mainly for outlines and finer details. Work the back-stitch when your cross stitch embroidery has been completed.

Always use one strand of stranded cotton less than in the cross stitch embroidery. For example, if three strands of stranded cotton were used to work the cross stitch, use two strands for the backstitching. If only one strand was used for the cross stitch, use one strand for the backstitching.

Backstitch is worked from hole to hole and can be stitched in diagonal, vertical or horizontal directions (Fig. 7). Take care not to pull the stitches too tight, otherwise the contrast of colour will be lost against the cross stitches. Finish off the threads as for cross stitch (Fig. 6).

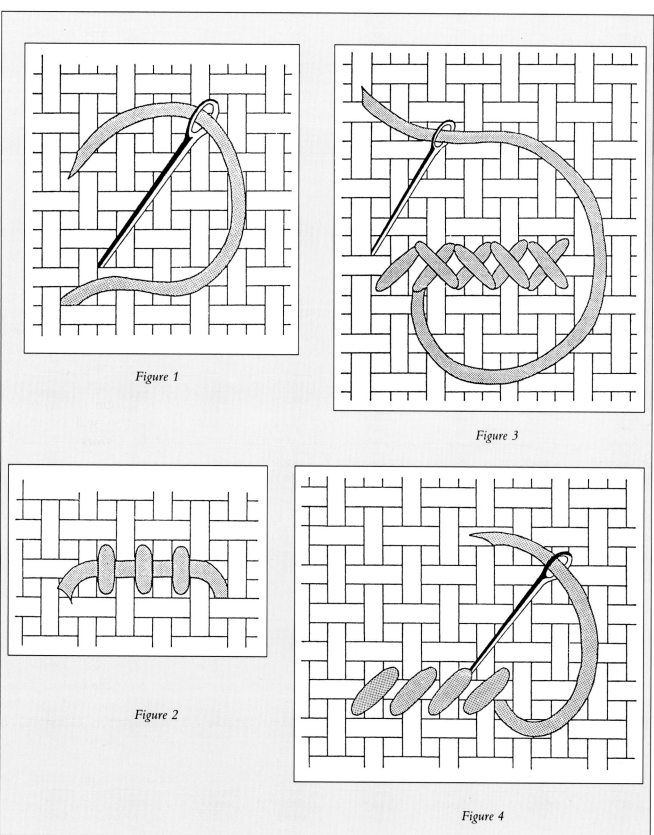

Figure 1

Figure 3

Figure 2

Figure 4

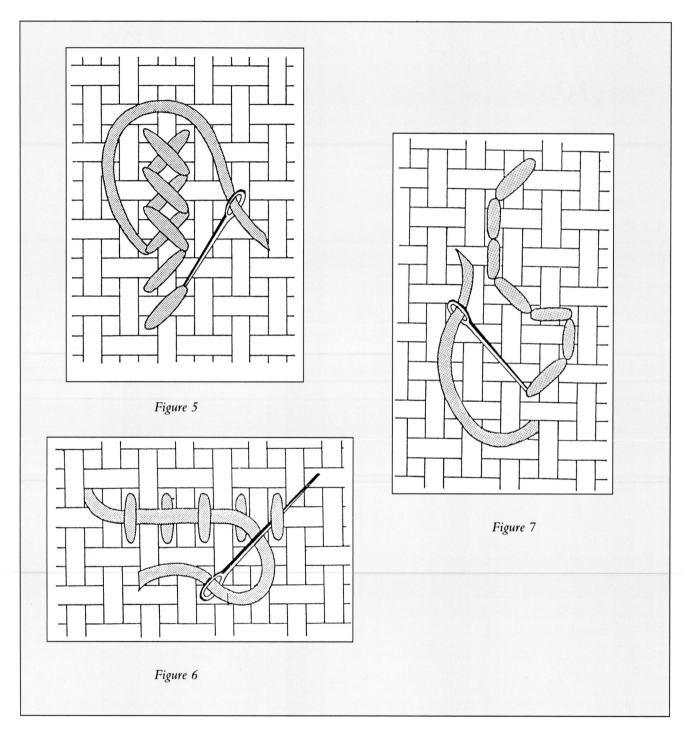

Figure 5

Figure 6

Figure 7

Completing a cross stitch project

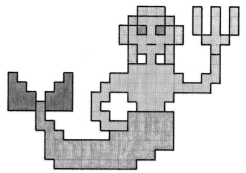

AFTER-CARE

When you have completed your cross stitch embroidery, it will need to be pressed. Place the embroidery right side down on a soft towel and cover the reverse with a thin, slightly damp cloth. Press with a hot iron.

You may find at some stage that your cross stitch embroidery needs to be laundered. This is no problem, just follow the simple advice recommended by DMC for their six-stranded cotton: wash embroidery separate from other laundry.

COTTON OR LINEN FABRIC	SYNTHETIC FABRIC
RECOMMENDED WASHING	
Wash in warm, soapy water. Rinse thoroughly. Squeeze without twisting and hang to dry. Iron on reverse side, under two layers of white linen.	Not recommended.
BLEACHING OR WHITENING AGENT	
Dilute the product according to the manufacturer's instructions. Pre-soak the embroidery in clear water, then soak for 5 minutes in a solution of 1 tablespoon disinfectant per quart of cold water. Rinse thoroughly in cold water.	Follow the instructions for cotton or linen if the white of the fabric is not of a high standard. If the fabric is pure white (white with a bluish tinge), do not use bleaching or whitening agent.
DRYCLEANING	
Avoid drycleaning. Some spot-removers (benzine, trichlorethylene) can be used for occasional small stains.	Not recommended, even for occasional small stains.

MOUNTING YOUR FINISHED EMBROIDERY

To mount your embroidery, you need to stretch it over a mounting board. Cut the board 2.5–4 centimetres (1–1½ inches) smaller all round than the embroidered fabric.

Place the embroidery face down on a clean, flat surface and place the mounting board centrally on top. Fold one edge of the fabric over the mounting board, ensuring that it is perfectly straight, and secure it with pins along the edge of the board. Secure the opposite edge in the same way, again making sure that the fabric is straight and taut on the board. Attach the edges of the fabric to the back of the mounting board with masking tape, then remove the pins. Repeat this procedure for the remaining two sides.

If you think this procedure is too fiddly to attempt, a company called Press-On Products Inc. produces a range of self-stick mounting boards, available in five different sizes from department stores and craft shops. These make the job easy. You simply cut the board to size as before, peel off the backing and lay your embroidered fabric on the board, making sure it is centred. When you are satisfied with the positioning, press down hard over the entire fabric surface. Tape the excess fabric to the back of the mounting board with masking tape.

Your embroidery picture is now ready to be framed. For the best results, take it to a professional framer. If you are having glass in the frame, non-reflective glass is best; although it is slightly more expensive, it is well worth it.

IDEAS FOR USING CROSS STITCH

The question many people ask is, 'What can I do with my finished embroidery?' Framing is the first thing most people think of, but there are many other ideas for more unusual projects. Cushions, table-linen, bedclothes and curtain tie-backs can all be decorated with cross stitch, and with the availability of waste canvas on the market clothing can also be decorated.

Framecraft Miniatures Ltd (see List of Suppliers, page 112) provides a whole range of items to mount cross stitch embroideries onto and into: miniature brass frames, trinket boxes, jewellery mounts, dressing-table sets, trays, cut-glass bowls, book-marks, bellpulls, paperweights, greetings cards and many other items.

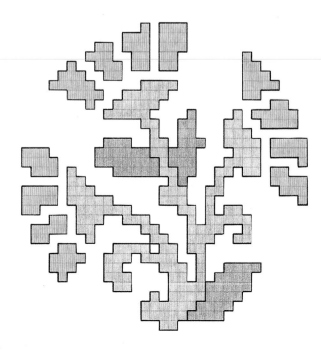

Stranded cotton shades and conversion chart

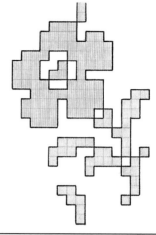

SHADE NAME	DMC	ANCHOR	COATS	MADEIRA
White	White	2	1001	White
Very dark lavender	208	110	4301	0804
Medium lavender	210	104	4304	0802
Medium mahogany brown	301	349	–	2306
Lemon yellow	307	289	2290	0104
Deep rose red	309	42	3284	0507
Black	310	403	8403	Black
Medium navy blue	311	148	–	1006
Light navy blue	312	147	7979	1005
Medium steel grey	317	400	8512	1714
Christmas red	321	47	3500	0510
Dark baby blue	322	978	7978	1004
Medium baby blue	334	161	7977	1003
Dark pink	335	42	3283	0506
Red	349	13	2335	0212
Dark peach	351	10	3012	0214
Dark mahogany brown	400	–	–	–
Very dark steel grey	413	401	8514	1713
Pale grey	415	398	8510	1803
Medium brown	433	371	5471	2008
Light brown	434	309	5000	2009
Very light brown	435	365	5371	2010
Tan brown	436	363	5943	2011
Dark Christmas red	498	47	–	0511
Very dark violet	550	101	4107	0714
Medium violet	553	98	4097	0712
Bright orange red	606	335	2334	0209
Very dark drab brown	610	906	–	2106
Drab brown	612	832	–	2108
Dark beaver grey	645	400	8500	1811
Bright Christmas red	666	46	3046	0210

SHADE NAME	DMC	ANCHOR	COATS	MADEIRA
Light old gold	676	891	2305	2208
Very light old gold	677	886	2300	2207
Dark old gold	680	901	5374	2210
Dark Kelly green	701	227	6226	1305
Kelly green	702	226	6239	1306
Topaz yellow	725	306	2298	0108
Very light topaz yellow	727	293	–	0110
Medium old gold	729	–	–	–
Very light tan	738	942	5375	2013
Tangerine orange	740	316	2099	0202
Medium tangerine orange	741	304	2314	0201
Dark yellow	743	297	2302	0113
Very light pearl grey	762	397	8510	1804
Very dark topaz brown	780	309	–	2214
Dark topaz brown	781	308	–	2213
Medium topaz brown	782	307	–	2212
Christmas gold	783	307	–	2211
Royal blue	797	132	7023	0912
Medium delft blue	799	130	7030	0910
Dark coffee brown	801	357	5475	2007
Delft blue	809	130	7021	0909
Medium garnet red	815	43	3000	0513
Garnet red	816	20	3410	0512
Dark navy blue	823	150	–	1008
Dark blue	825	162	–	1011
Medium blue	826	161	–	1012
Light golden wheat yellow	834	874	–	2204
Very dark beaver grey	844	401	–	1810
Dark carnation red	89	29	–	0411
Very dark coffee brown	898	360	5476	2006
Medium pink	899	27	3282	0505
Dark emerald green	910	228	6031	1301
Light emerald green	912	209	6225	1212
Dark dusty rose pink	961	40	–	0610
Very light dusty rose pink	963	48	–	0608
Light pumpkin orange	970	316	2327	0204
Deep canary yellow	972	303	–	0107
Bright canary yellow	973	297	–	0105
Medium golden brown	976	309	–	2302
Dark forest green	987	245	6258	1403
Light forest green	989	256	6266	1401

Shade name	DMC	Anchor	Coats	Madeira
Aquamarine	992	187	6186	1202
Medium electric blue	996	433	7001	1103
Very dark brown-grey	3021	382	5395	1904
Brown-grey	3022	8581	–	1903
Medium beige	3032	–	–	–
Pale golden wheat	3047	886	2300	2205
Very light golden yellow	3078	292	2292	0102
Baby blue	3325	159	7976	1002
Pink	3326,	26	3126	0504
Medium salmon red	3328	11	3071	0408
Very dark yellow green	3345	268	6258	1406
Dark yellow green	3346	257	6258	1407
Medium yellow green	3347	267	6266	1408
Light yellow green	3348	265	6266	1409
Dark antique rose pink	3350	69	–	0603
Antique rose pink	3354	75	–	0608
Light loden green	3364	843	6010	1603
Very dark forest brown	3371	382	–	2004
Medium fuchsia purple	3607	87	–	0708
Fuchsia purple	3608	86	–	0709
Light fuchsia purple	3609	85	–	0710
Dark mauve	3685	70	–	0602
Mauve	3687	68	–	0604
Medium mauve	3688	66	–	0605
Light mauve	3689	73	–	0607
Water melon orange	3705	35	–	0410
Medium water melon orange	3706	33	–	0409
Light water melon orange	3708	31	–	0408

Flowers
& plants

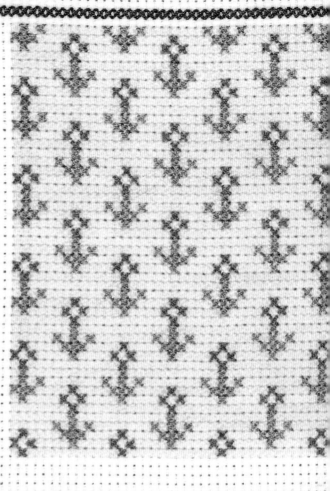

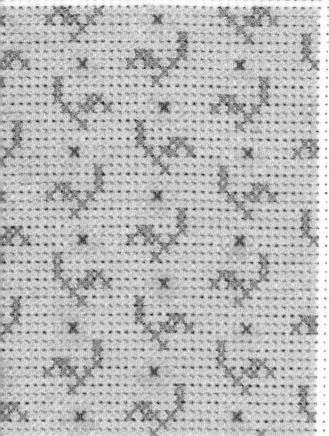

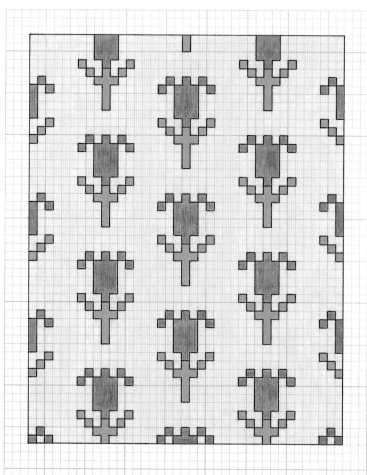

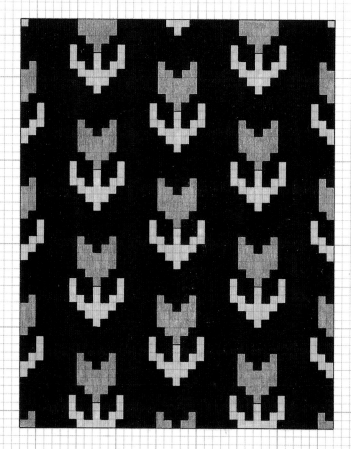

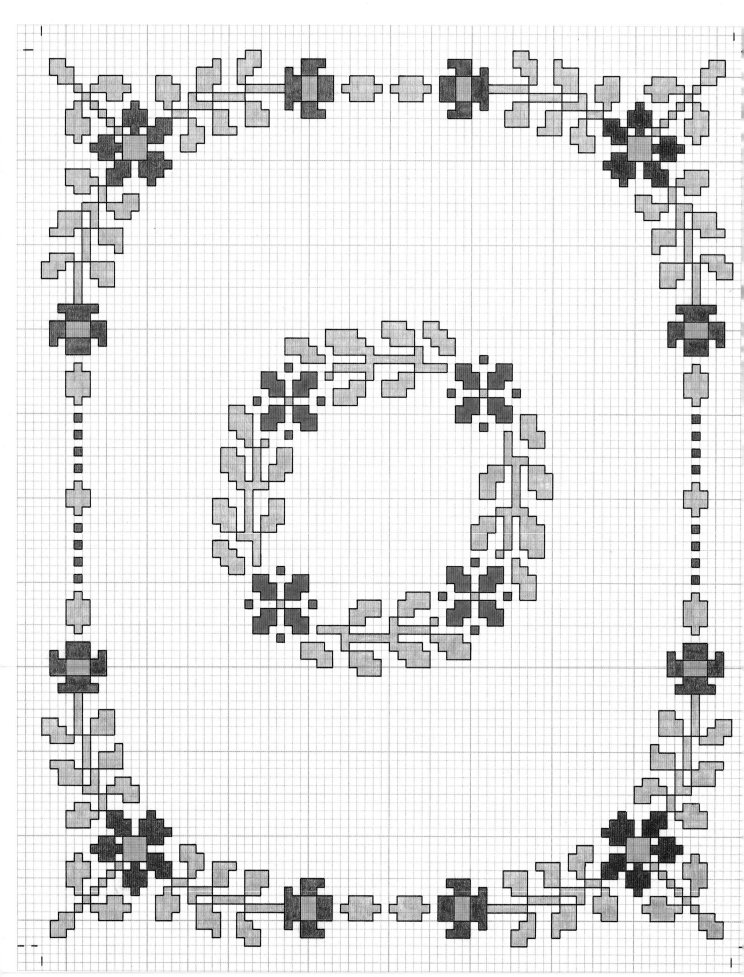

31

Animals
& pets

Rough collie

German shepherd

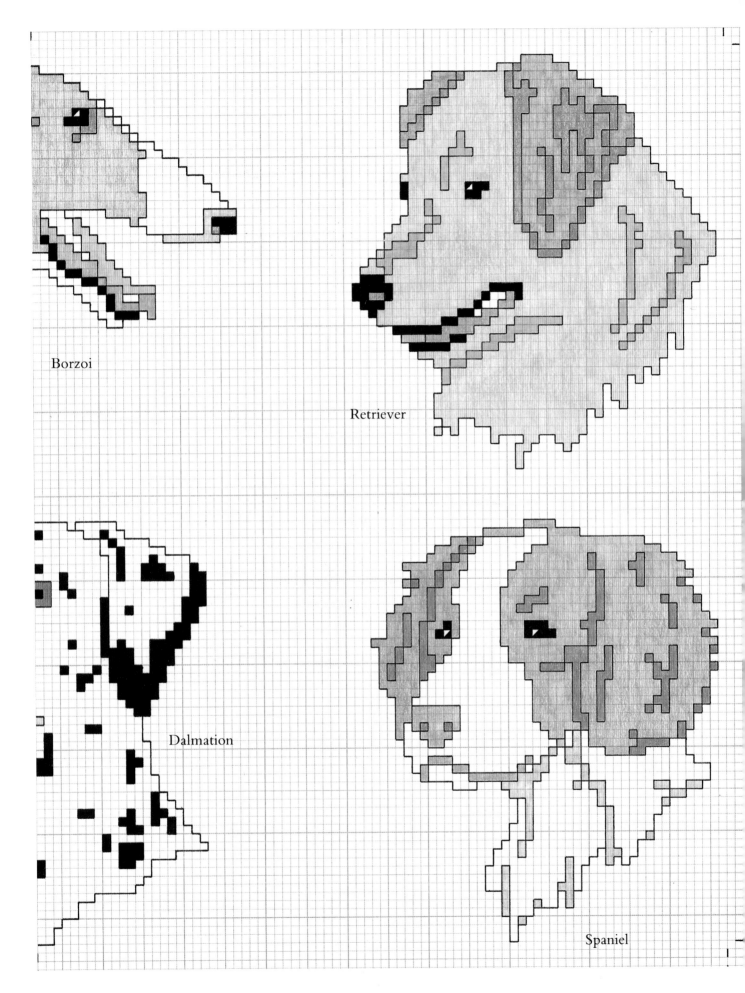

Borzoi

Retriever

Dalmation

Spaniel

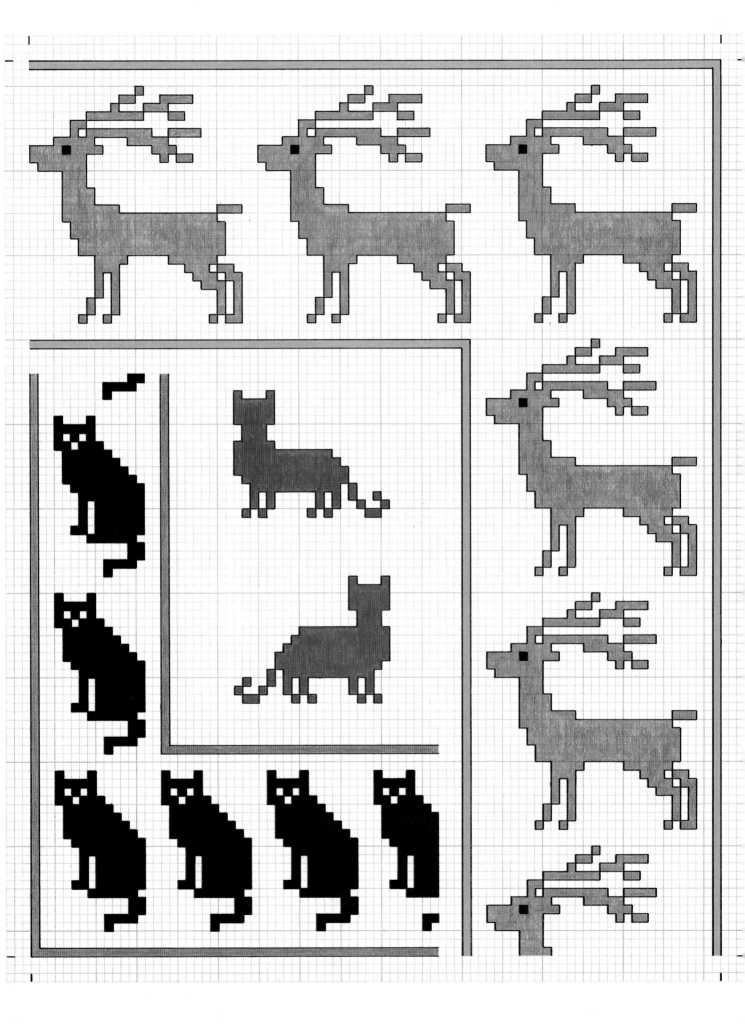

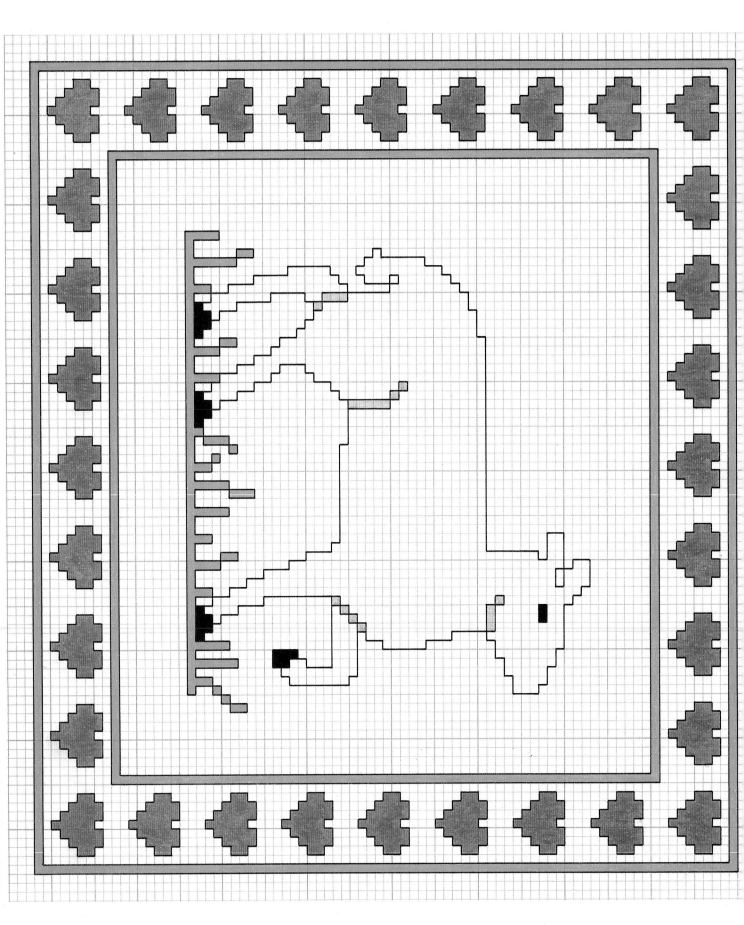

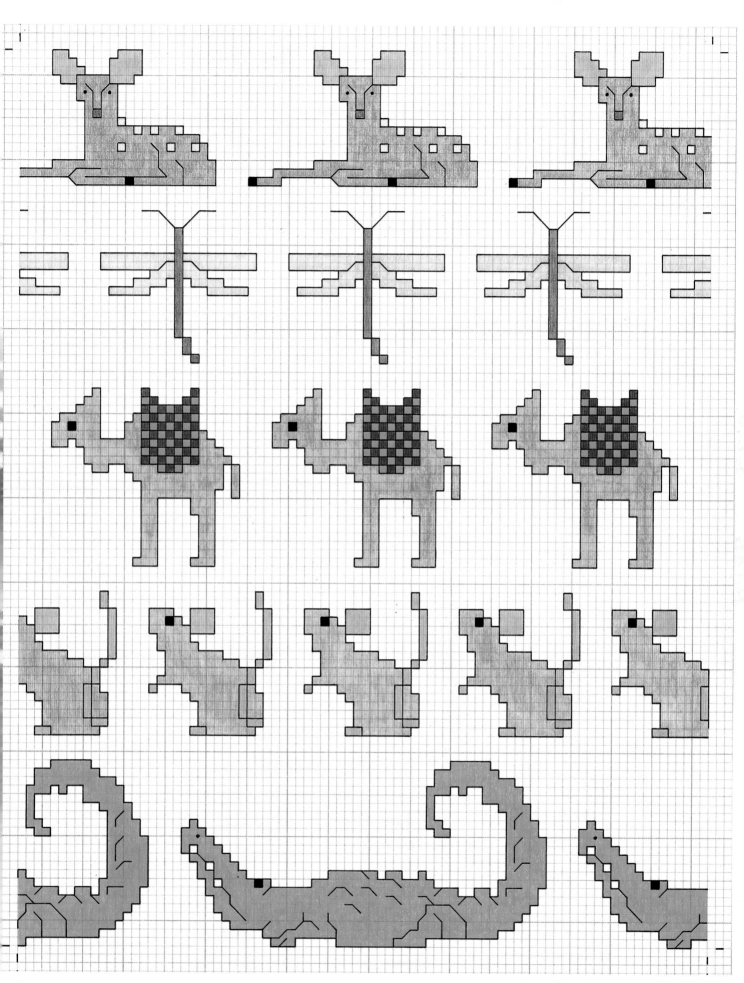

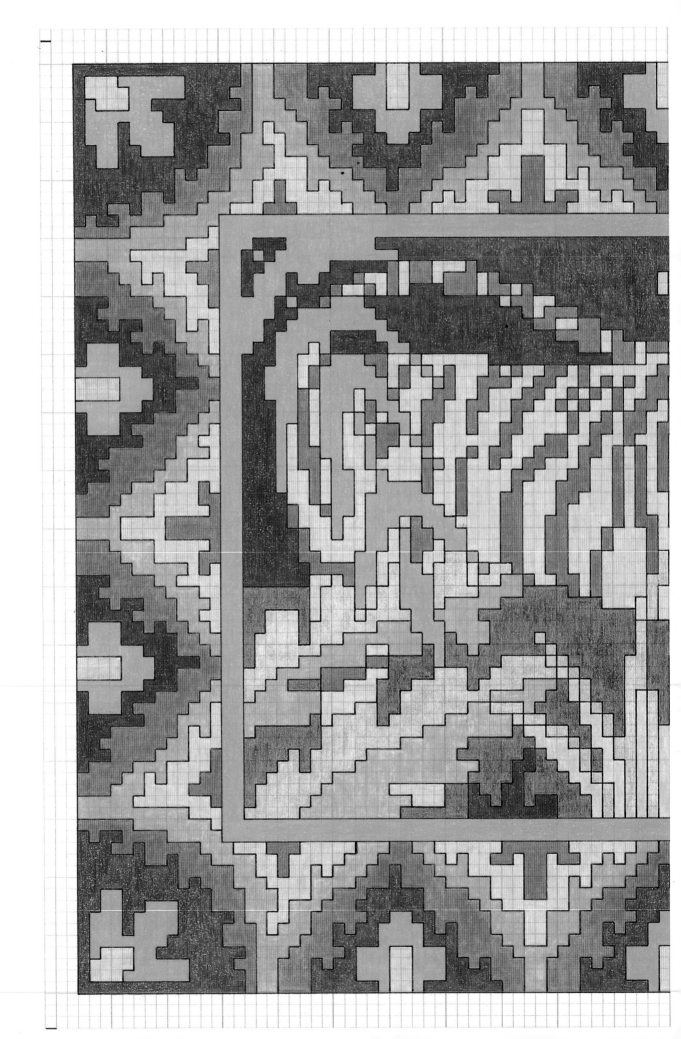

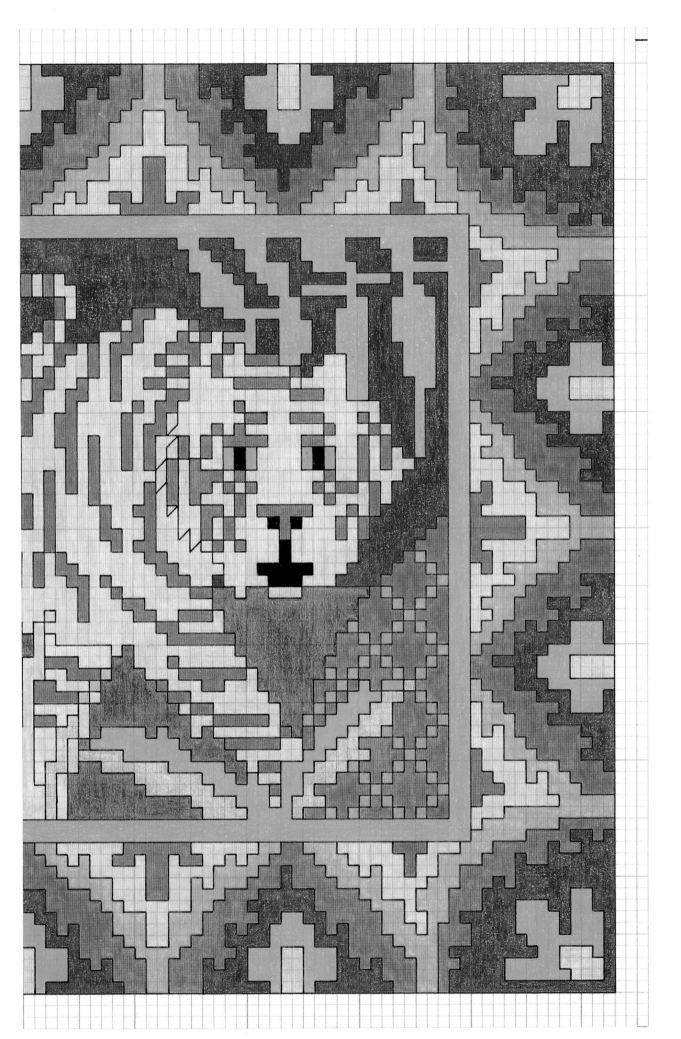

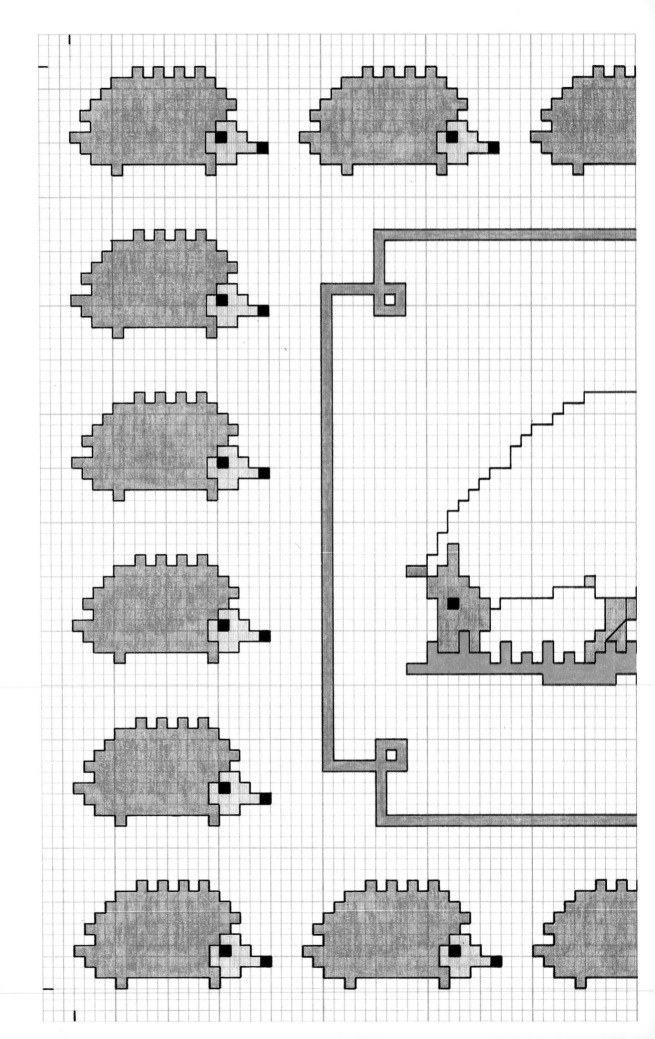

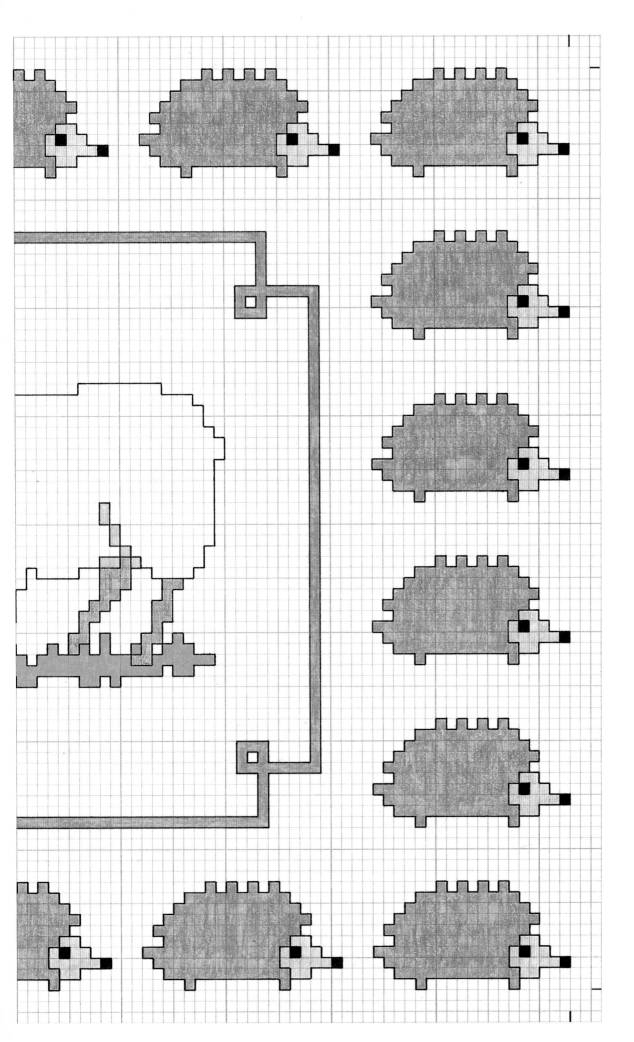

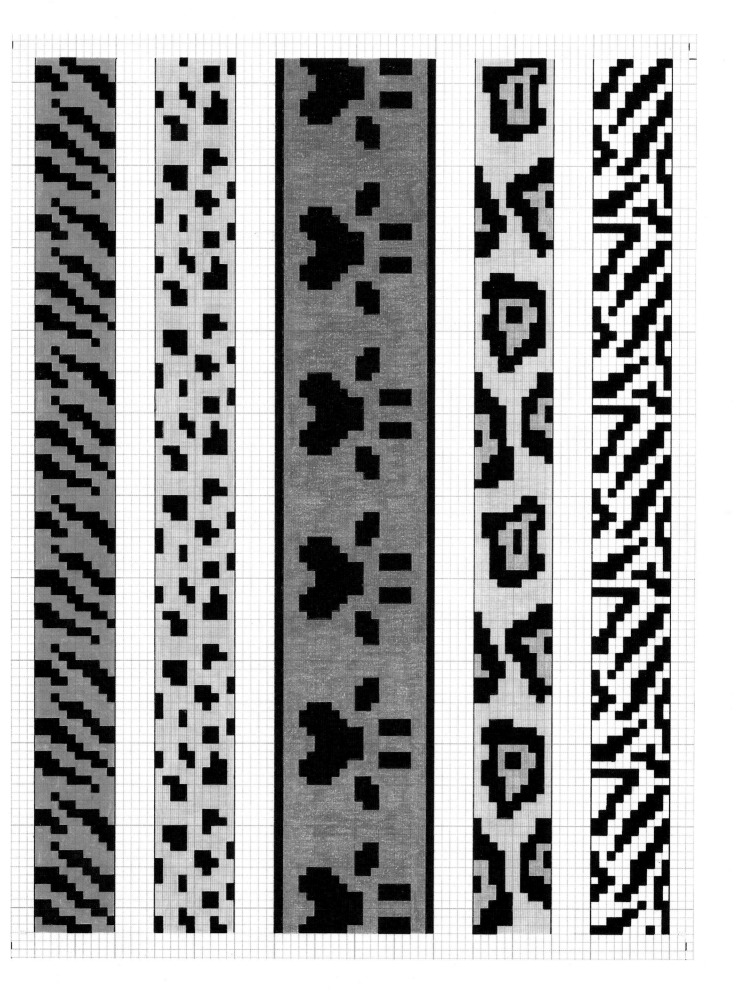

Birds

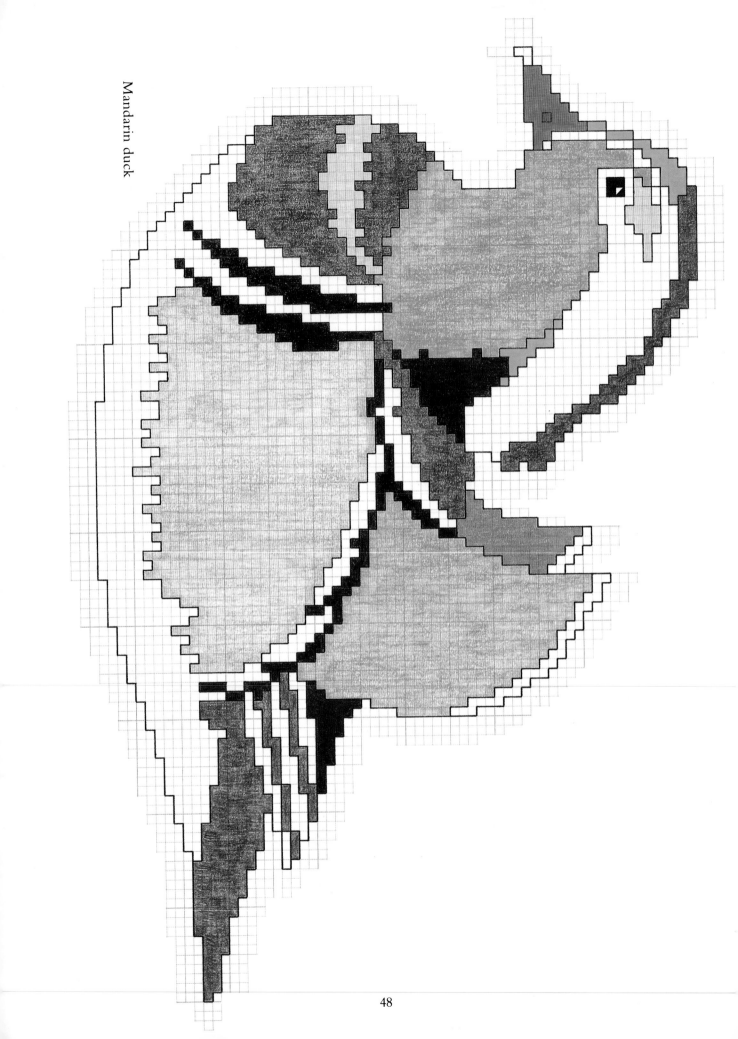

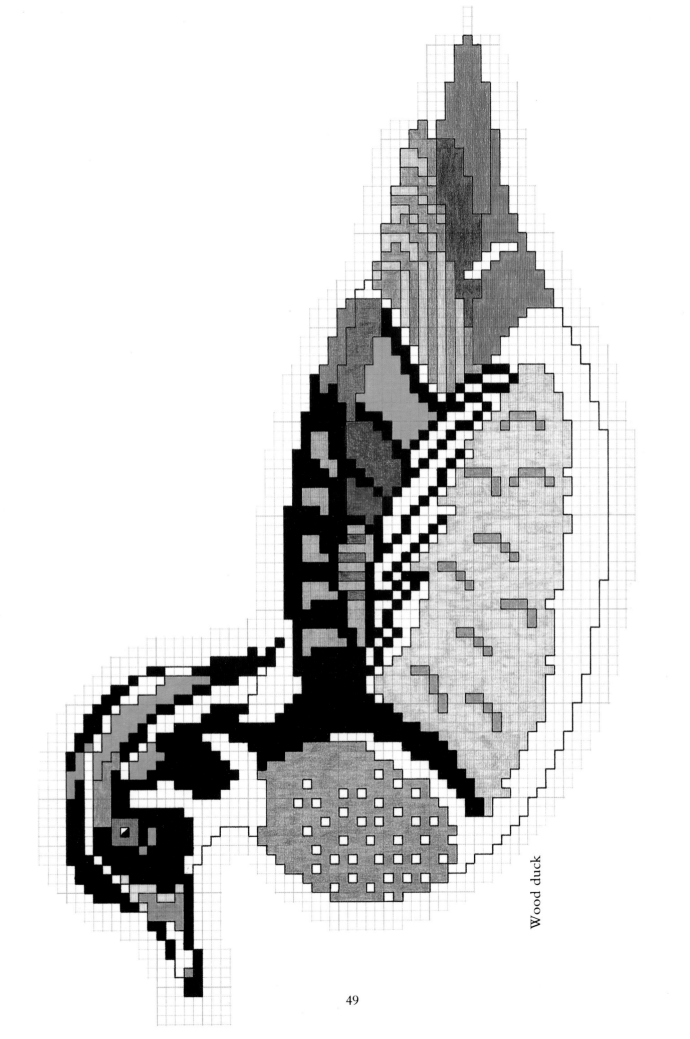

Wood duck

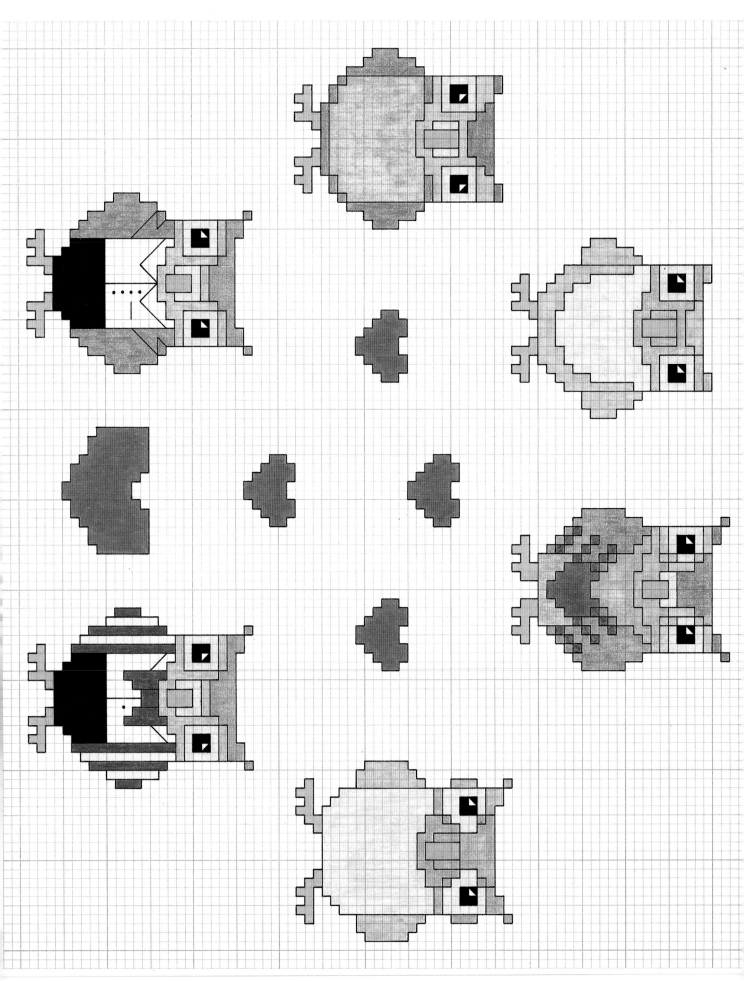

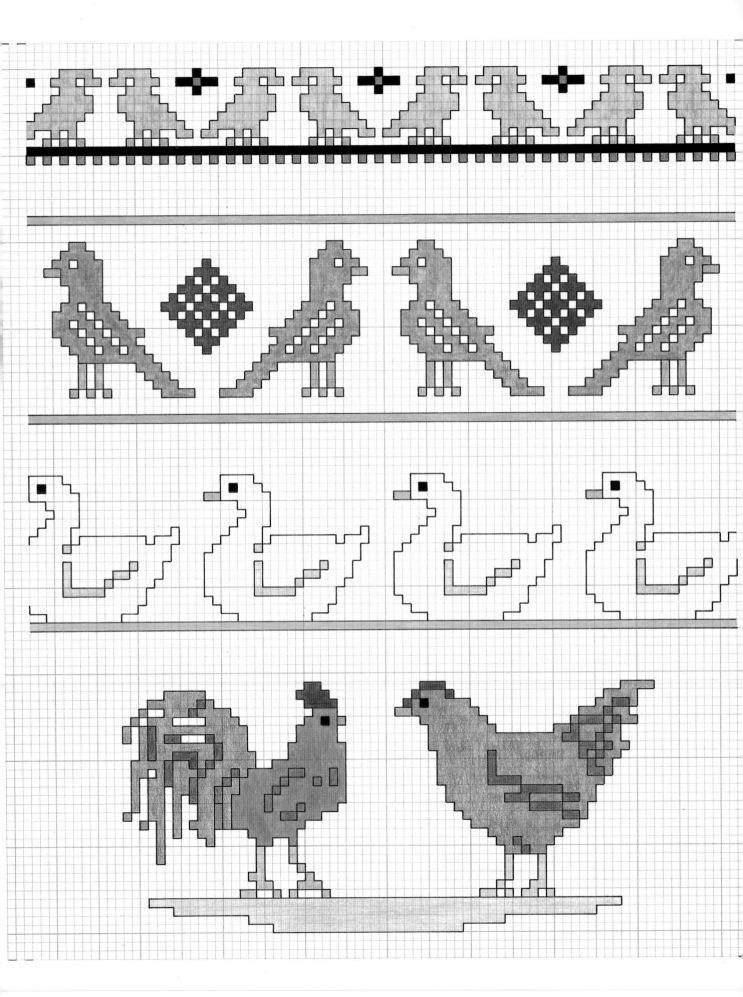

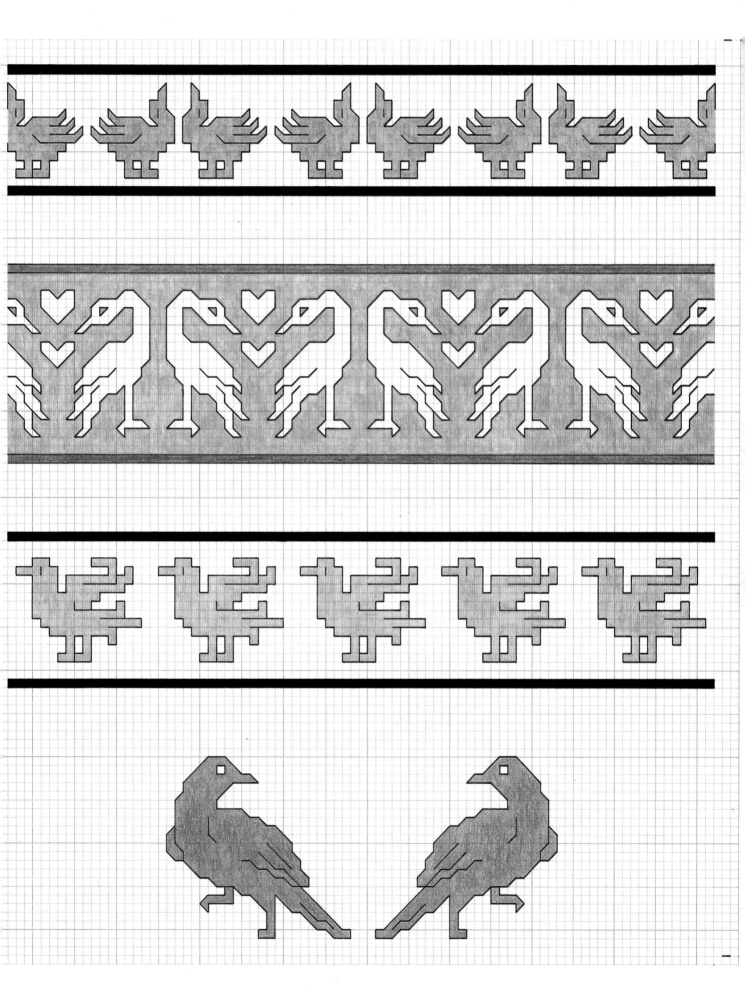

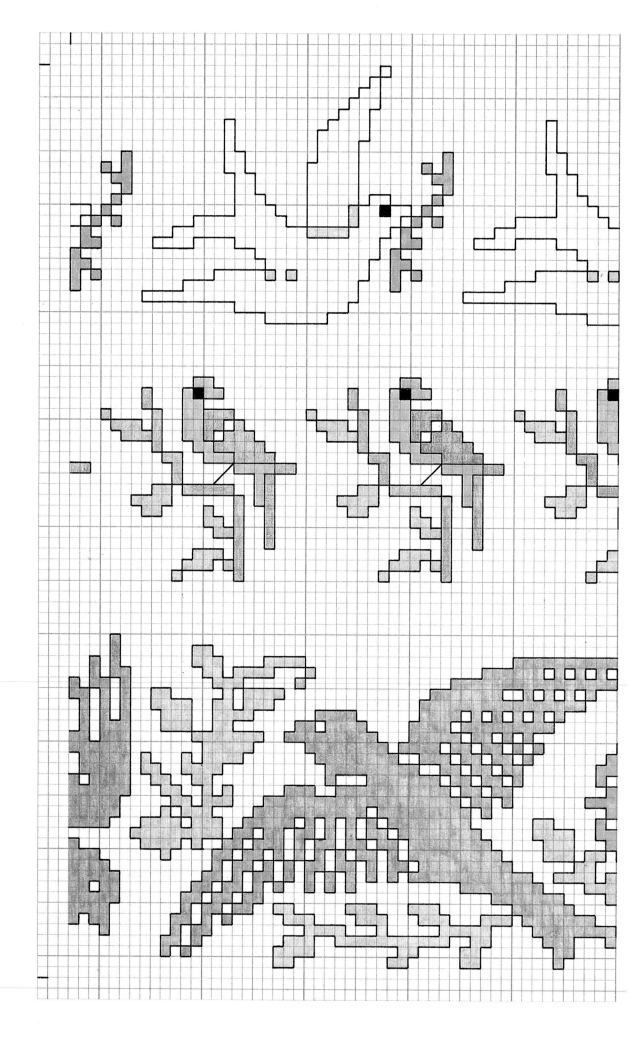

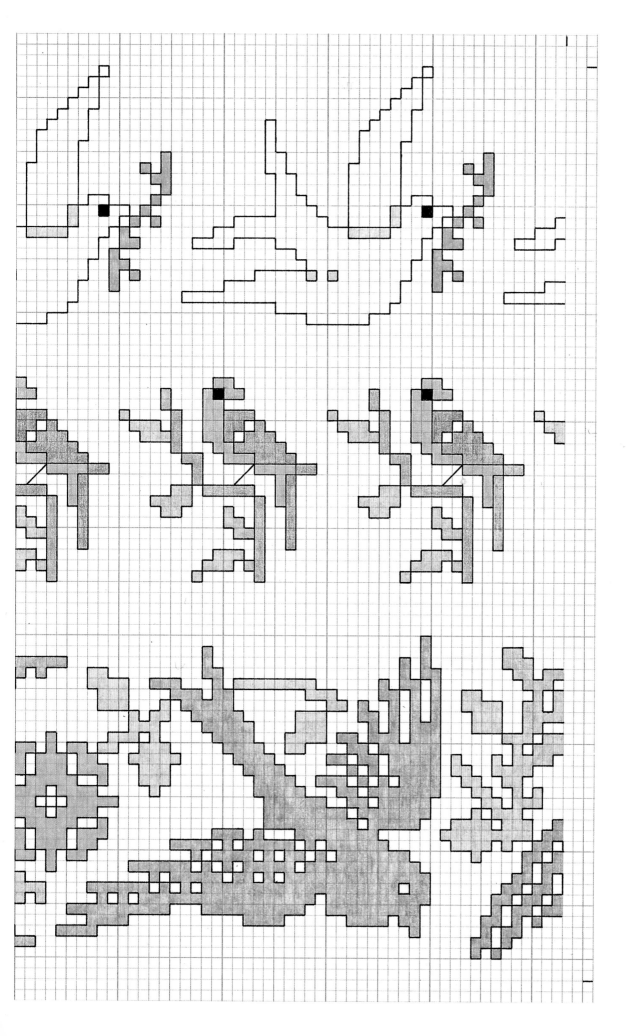

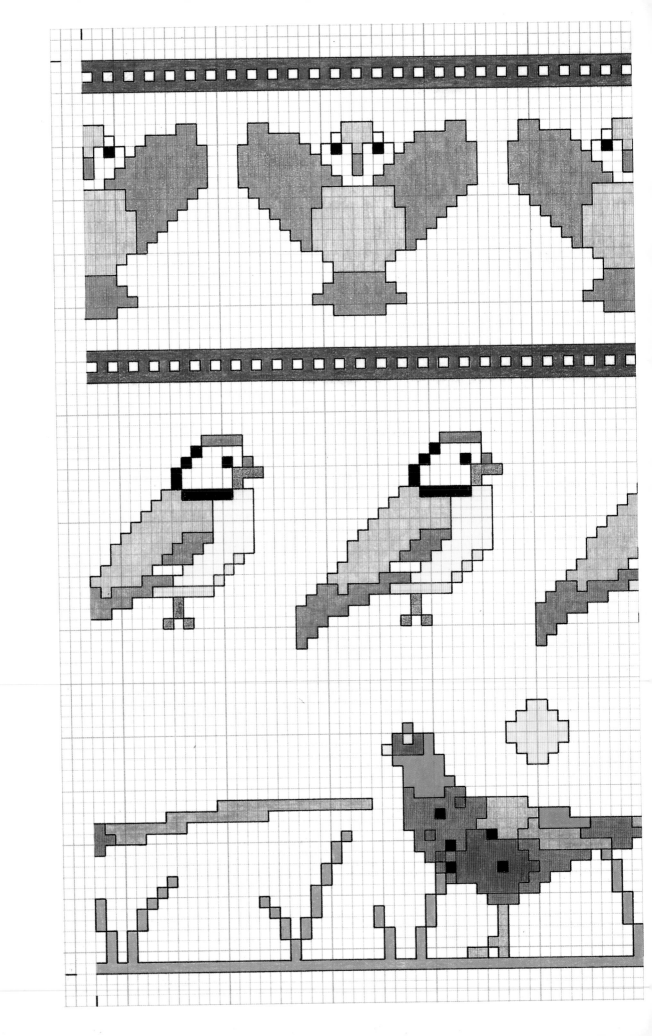

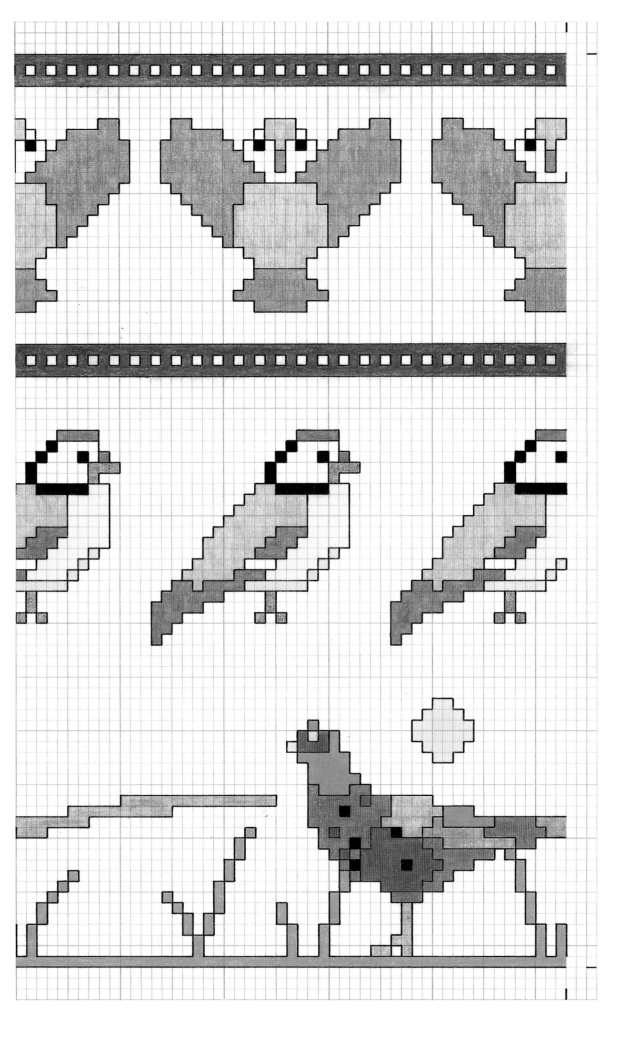

Historical
designs

Lion

Castle

Griffin

Ship

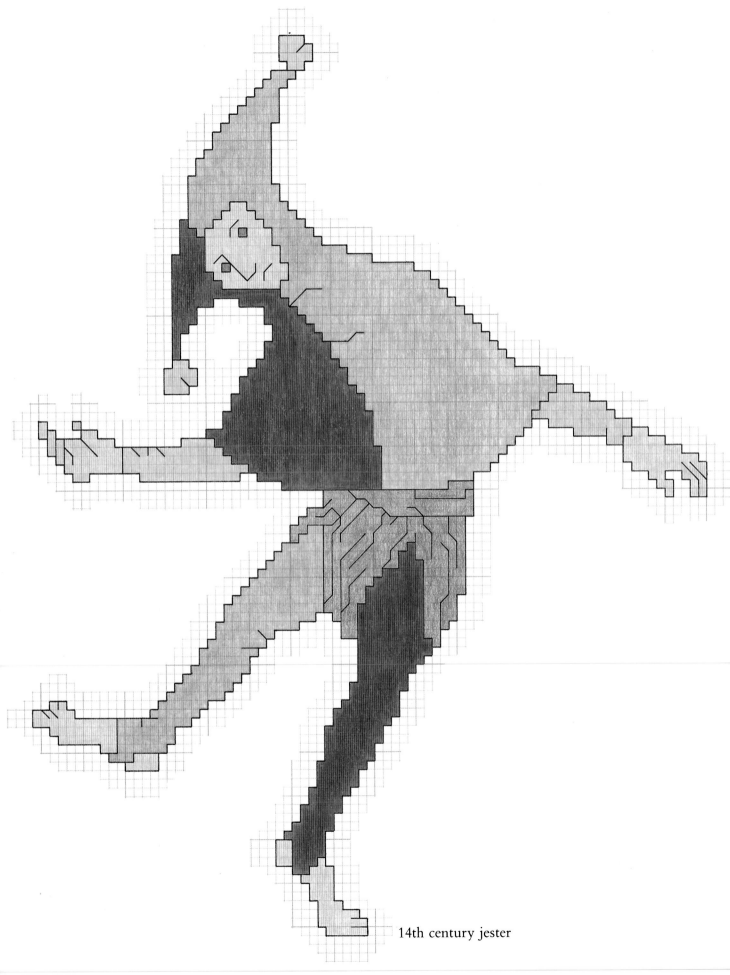

14th century jester

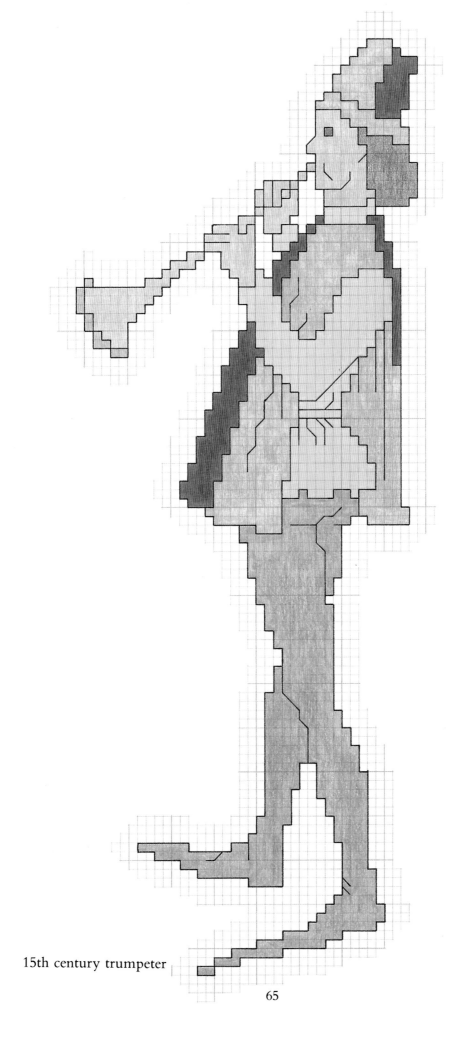

15th century trumpeter

Traditional Indian design

Traditional Indian design

Lion and unicorn

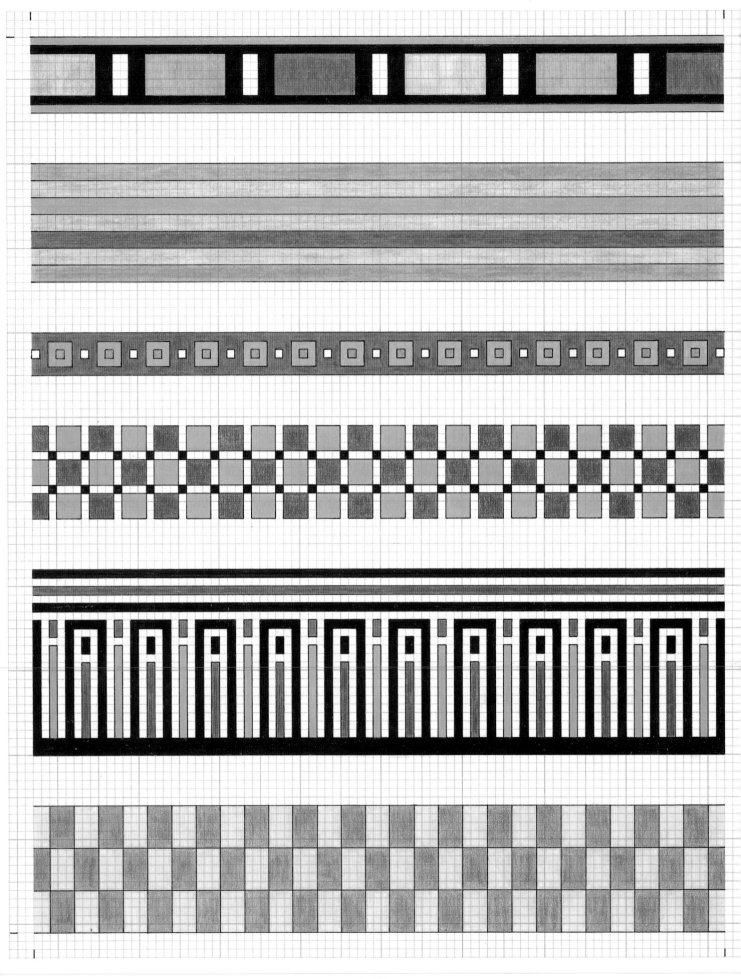

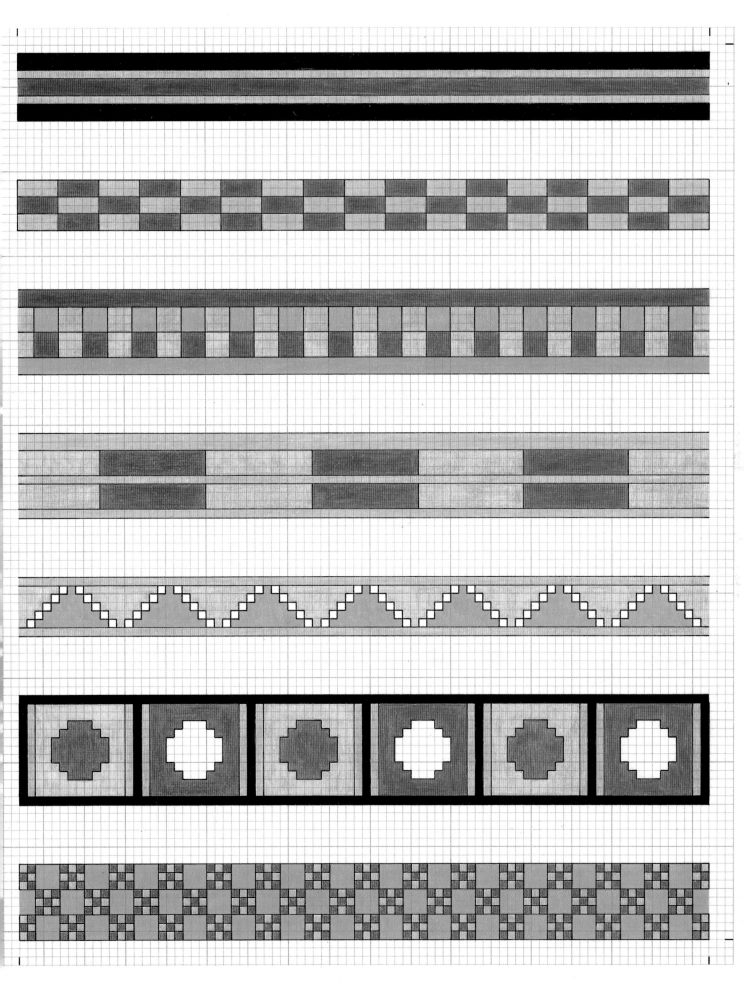

Traditional
samplers

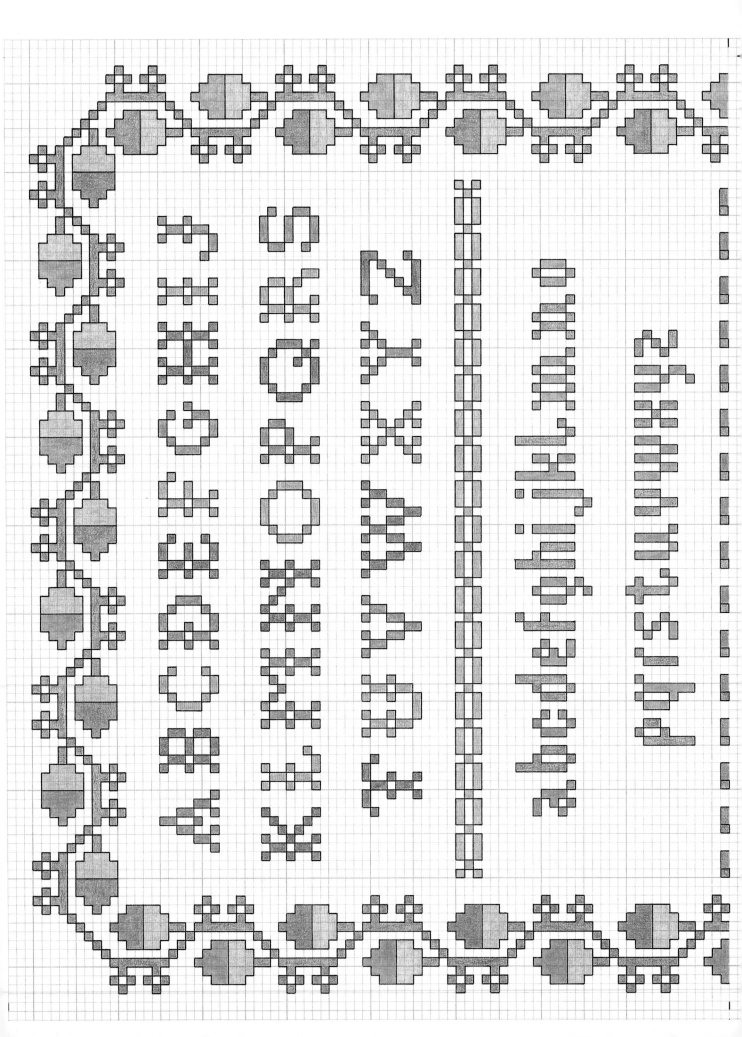

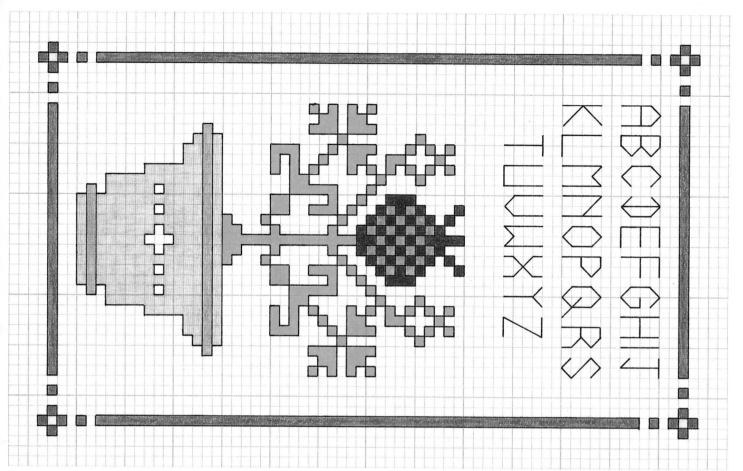

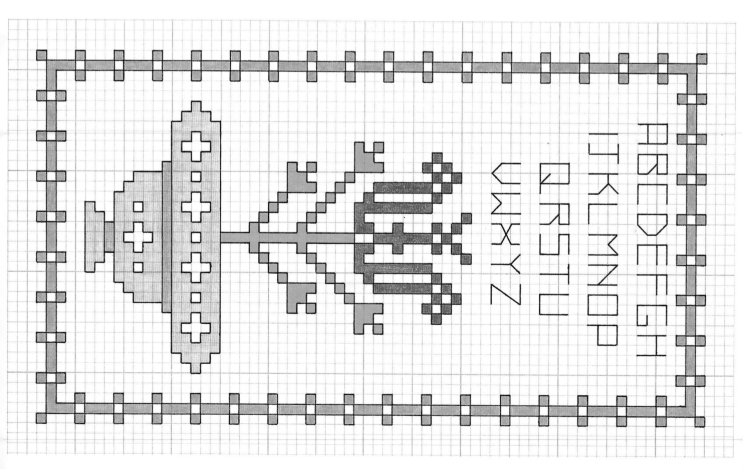

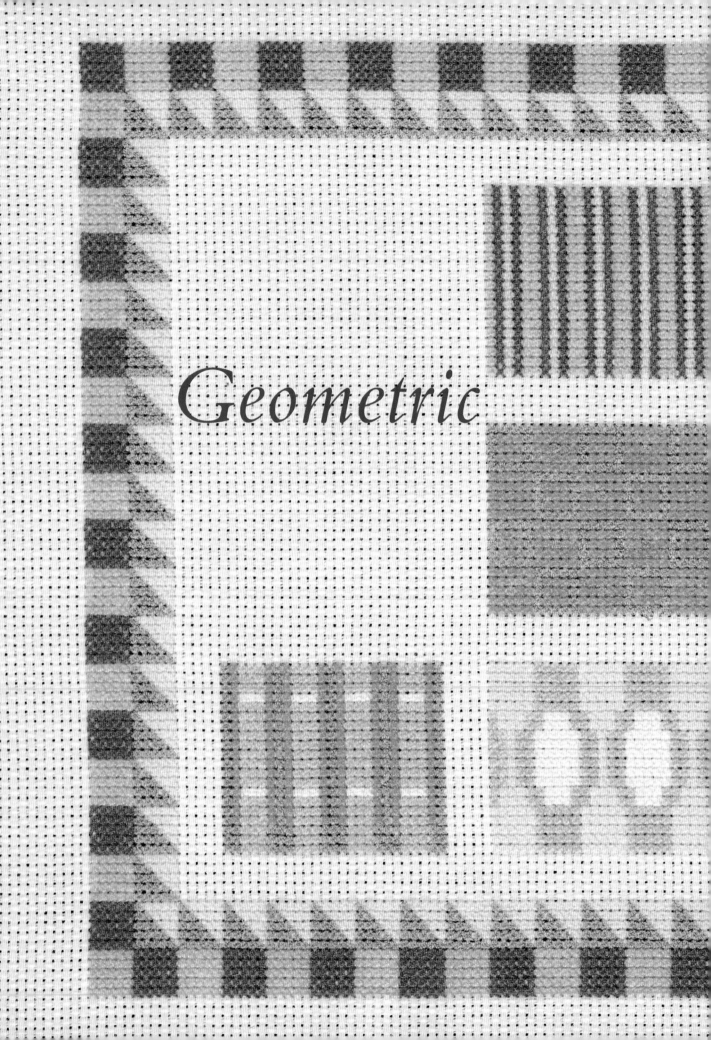

Geometric

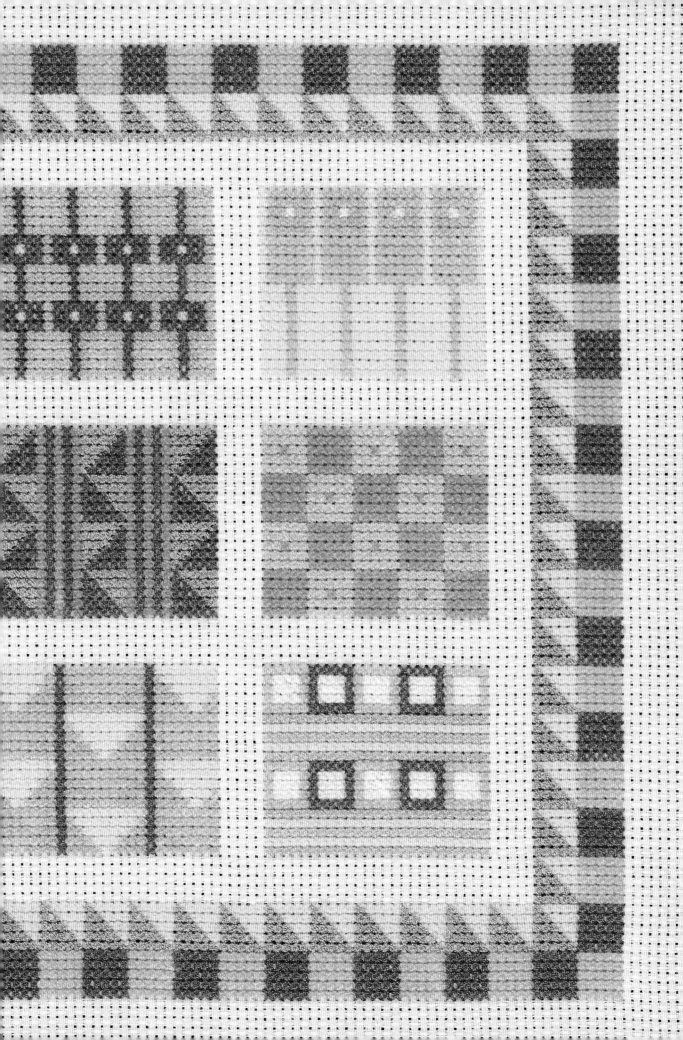

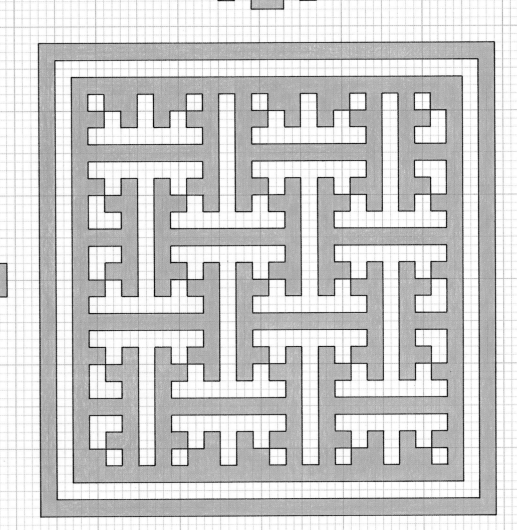
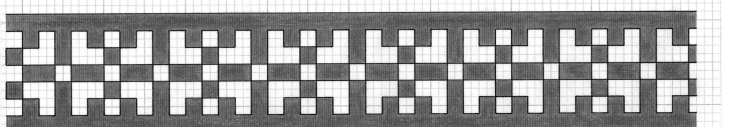

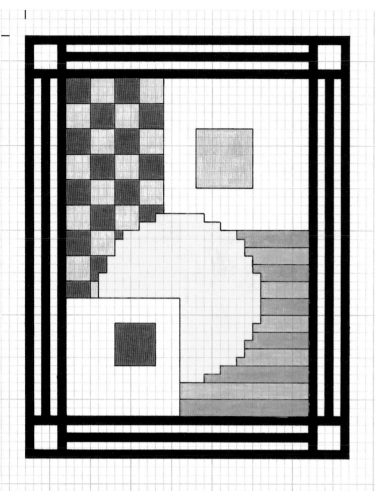

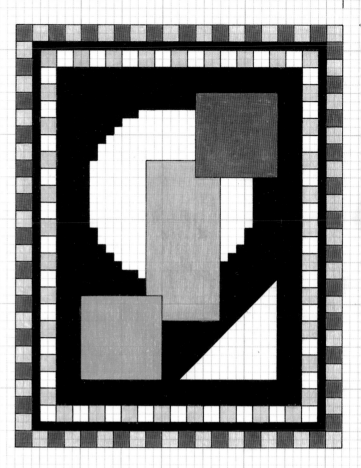

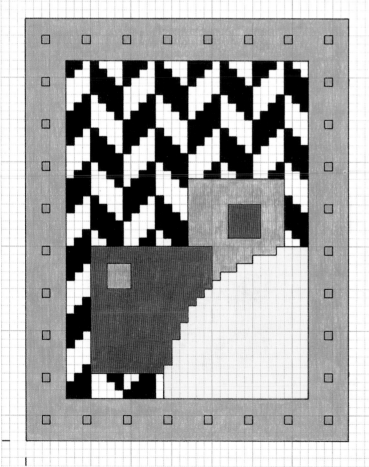

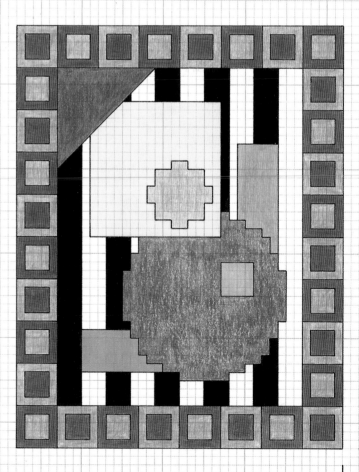

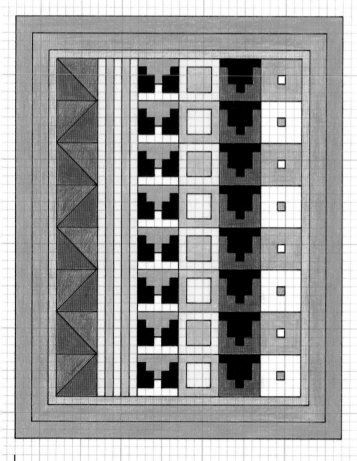

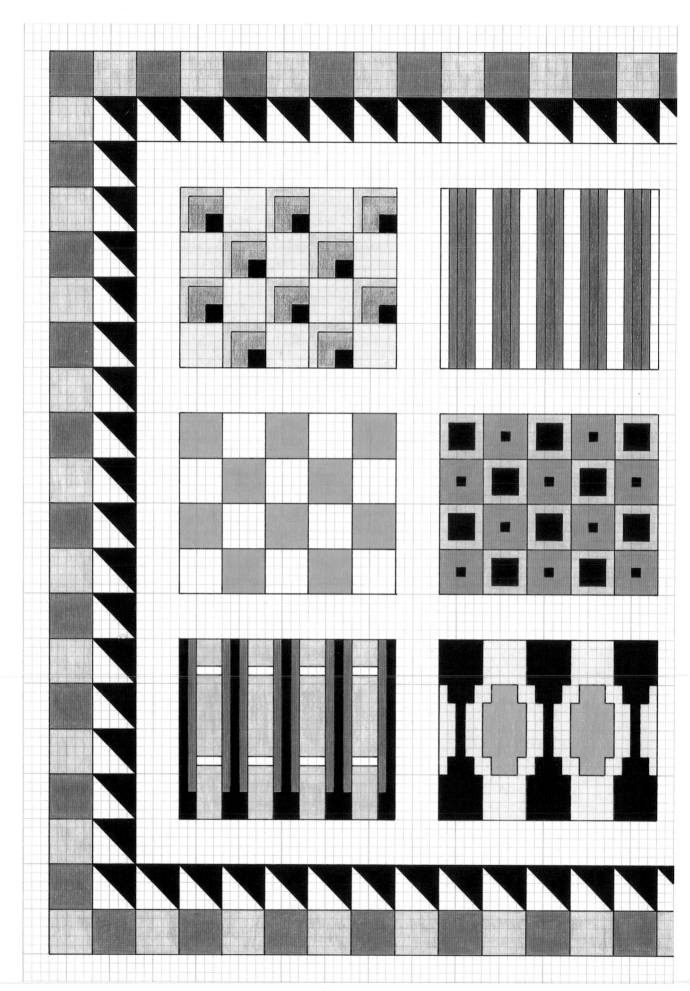

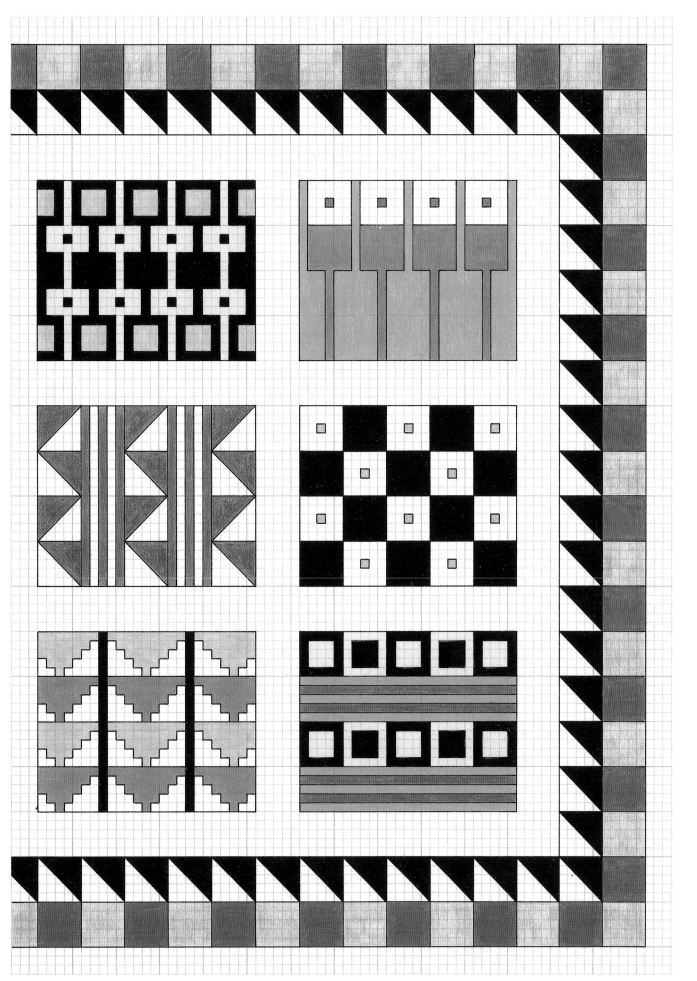

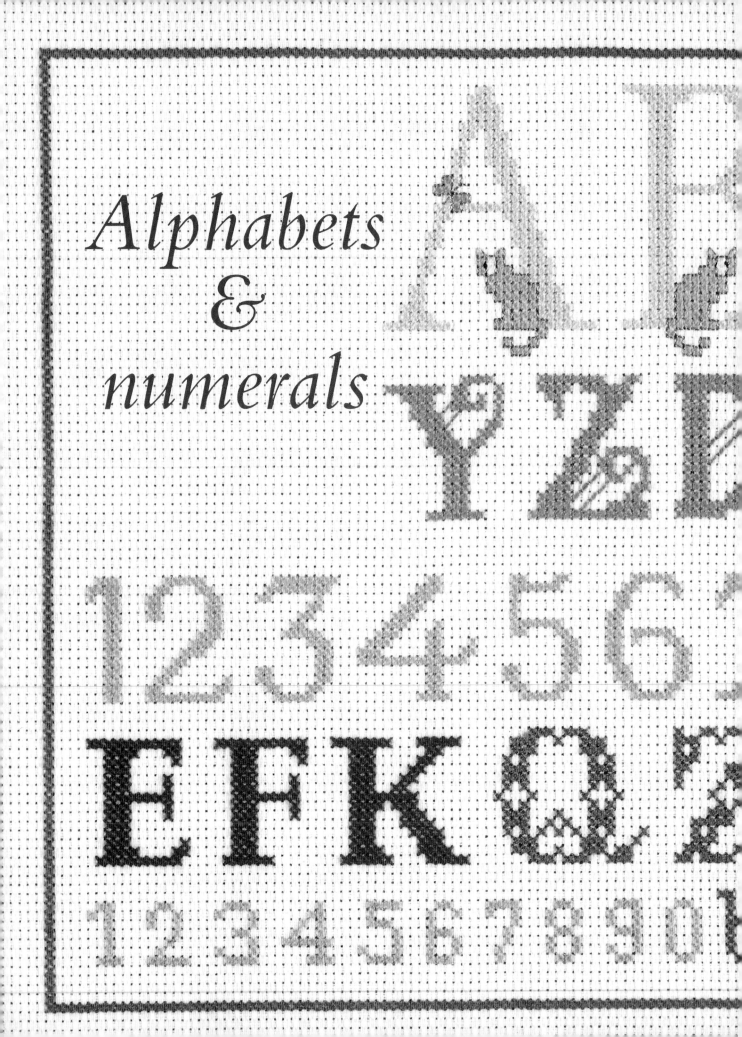

*Alphabets
&
numerals*

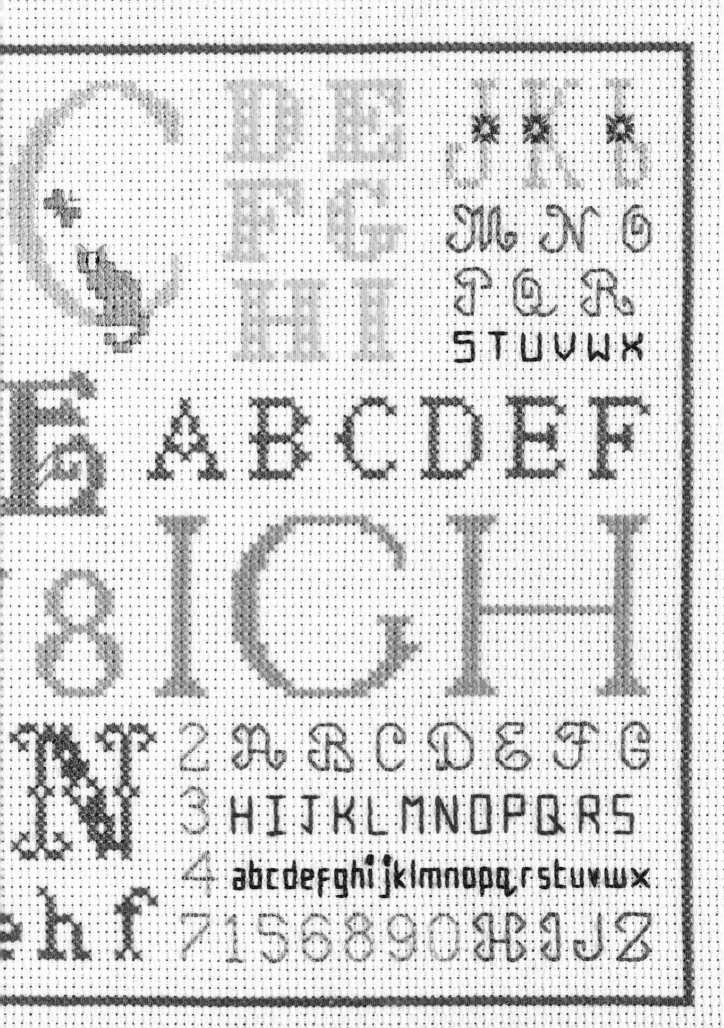

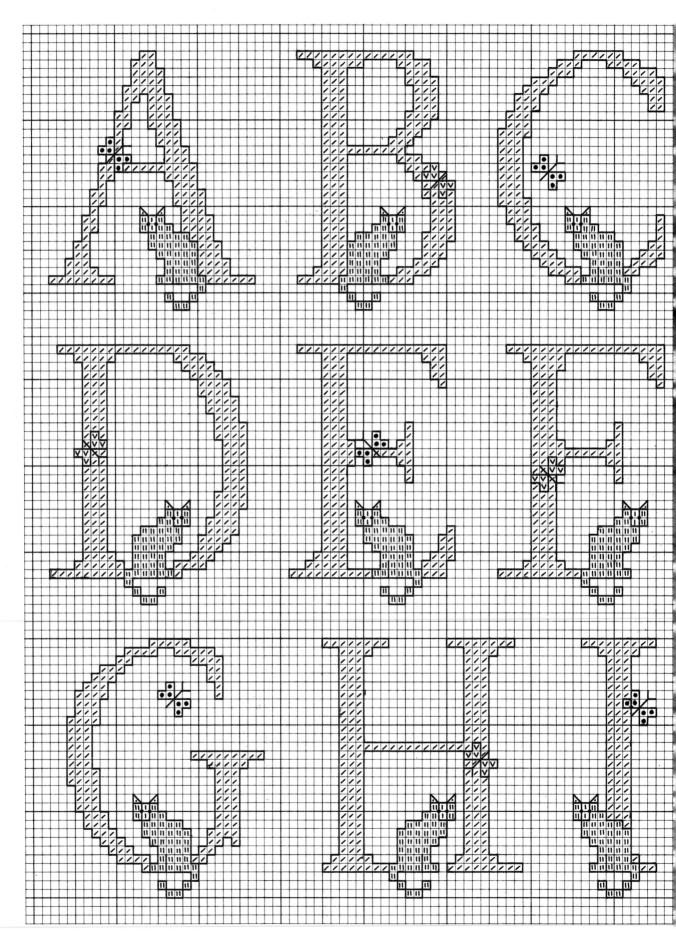

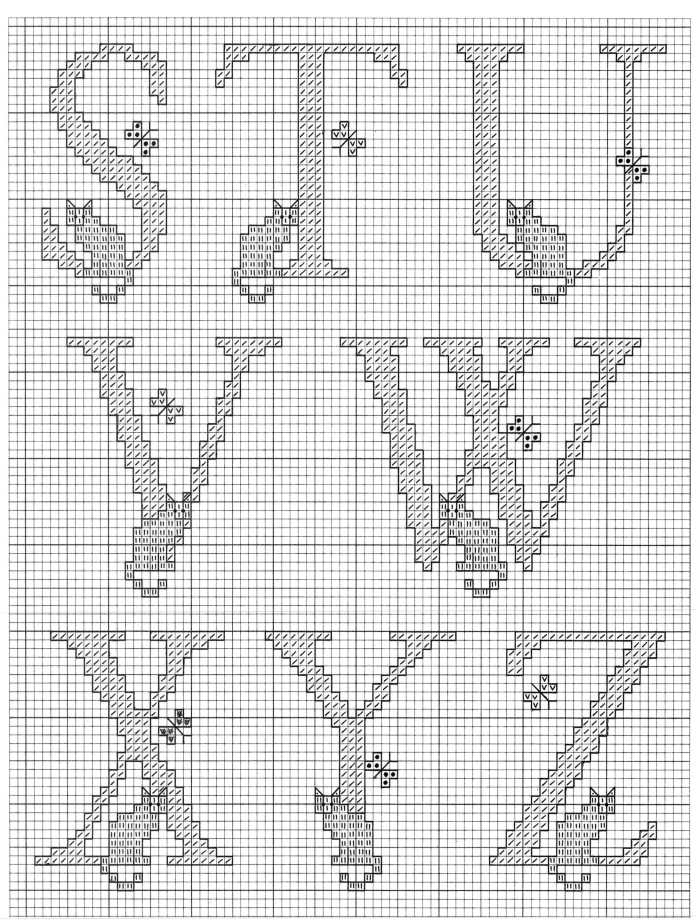

ABCDEFG
HIJKLMN
OPQRST
UVWXYZ

abcdefghi
jklmnopqrs
tuvwxyz

1234567890

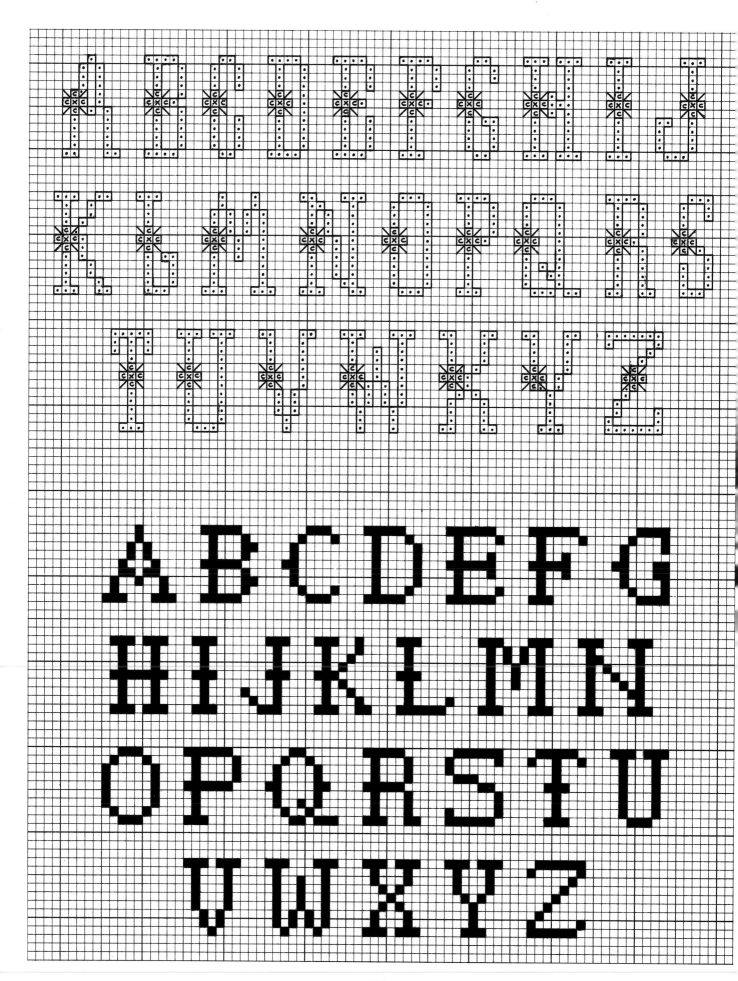

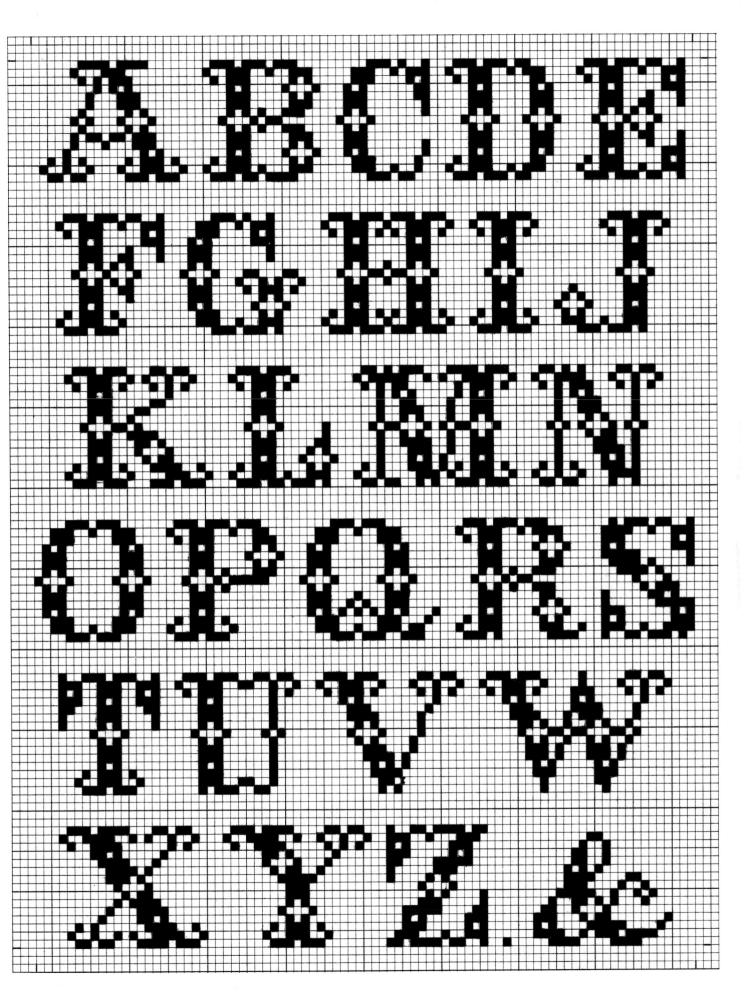

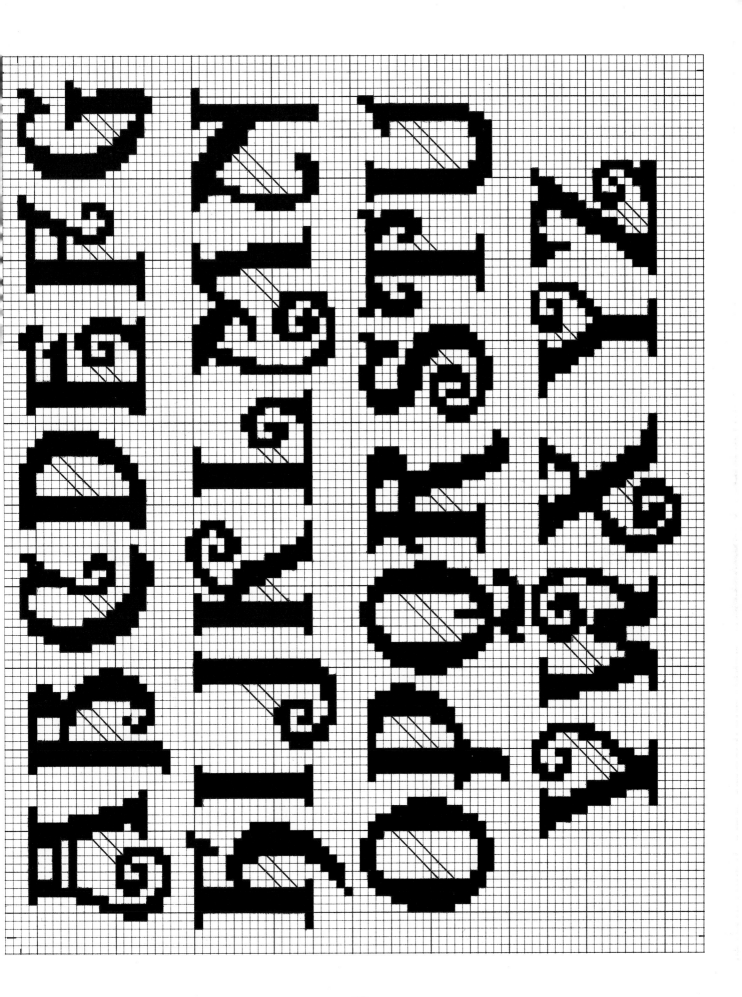

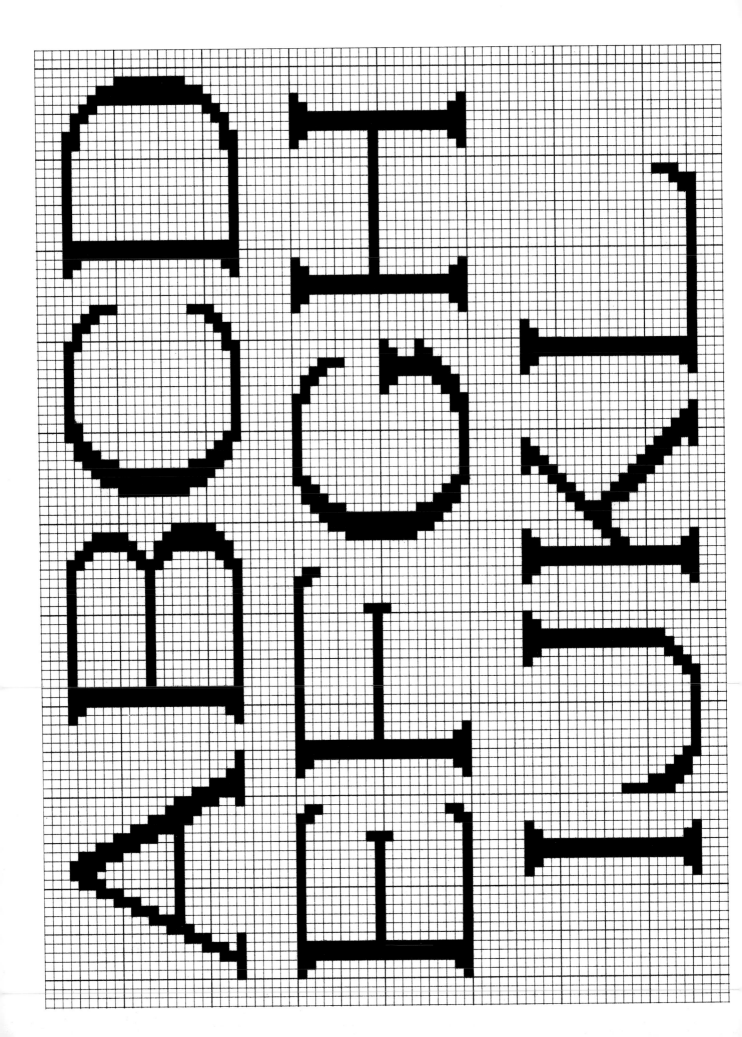

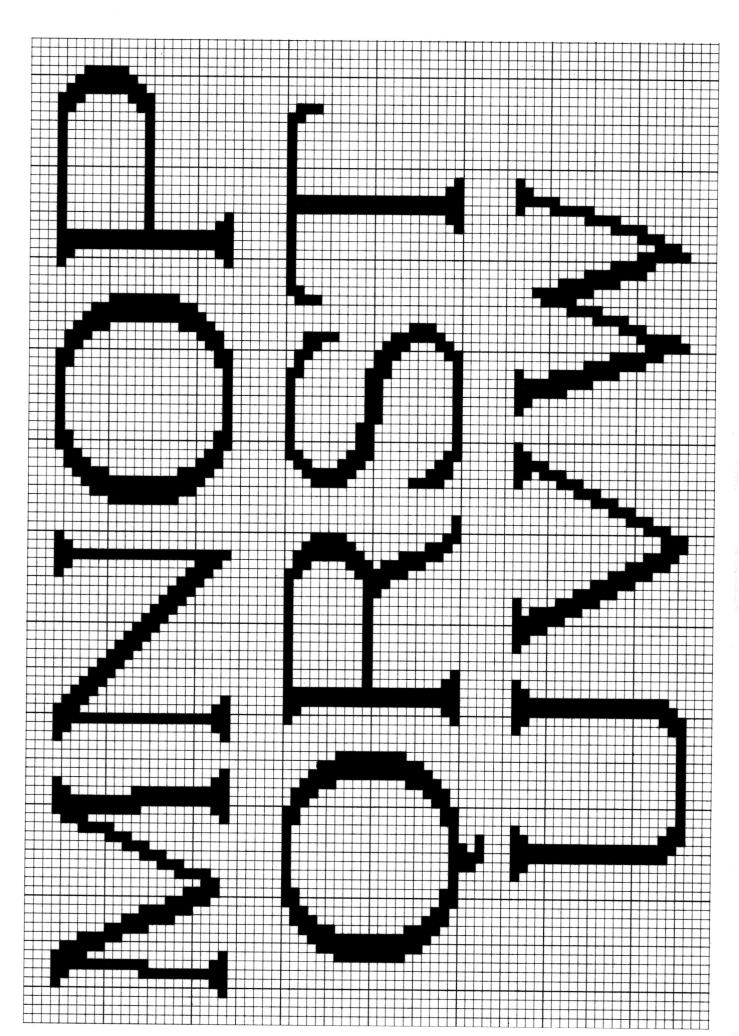

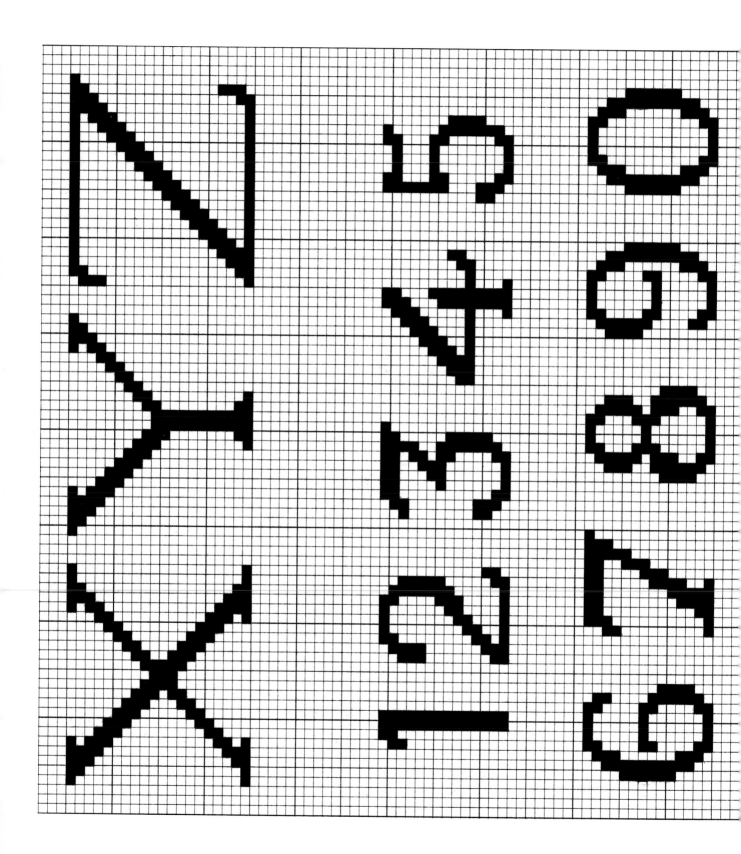

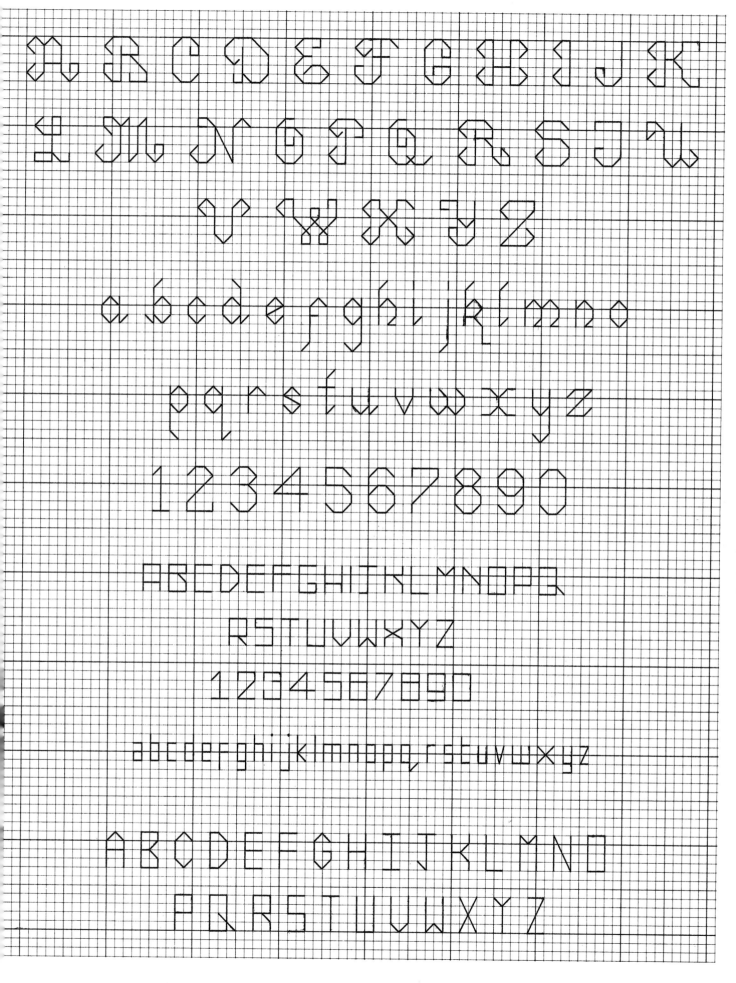

ABCDEFGHIJK
LMNOPQRSTU
VWXYZ

a b c d e f g h i j k l m n o

p q r s t u v w x y z

1234567890

ABCDEFGHIJKLMNOPQ
RSTUVWXYZ
1234567890

abcdefghijklmnopqrstuvwxyz

ABCDEFGHIJKLMNO
PQRSTUVWXYZ

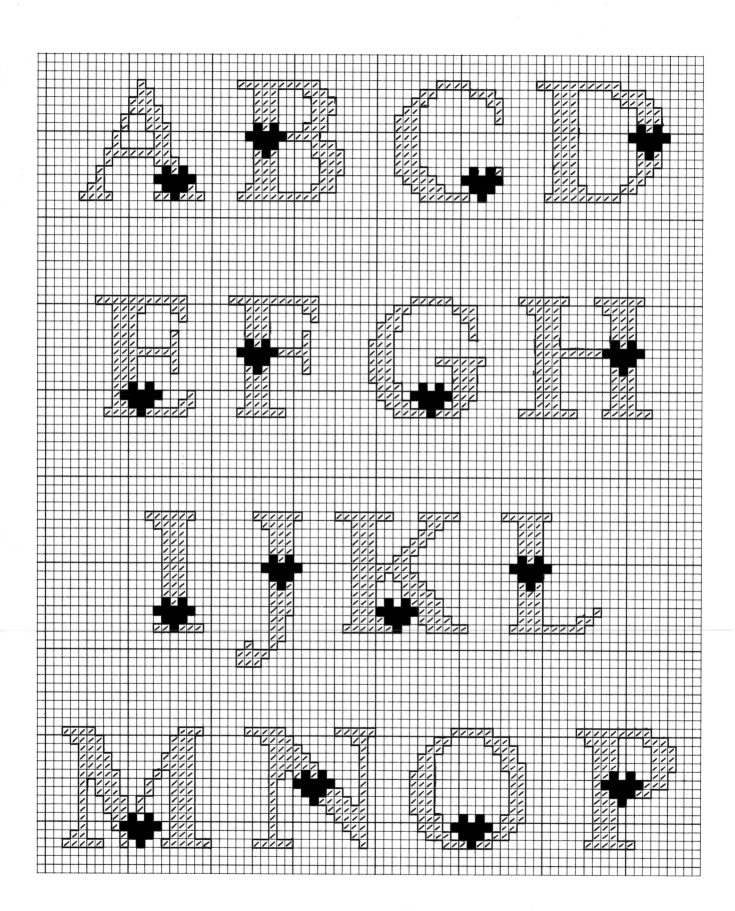

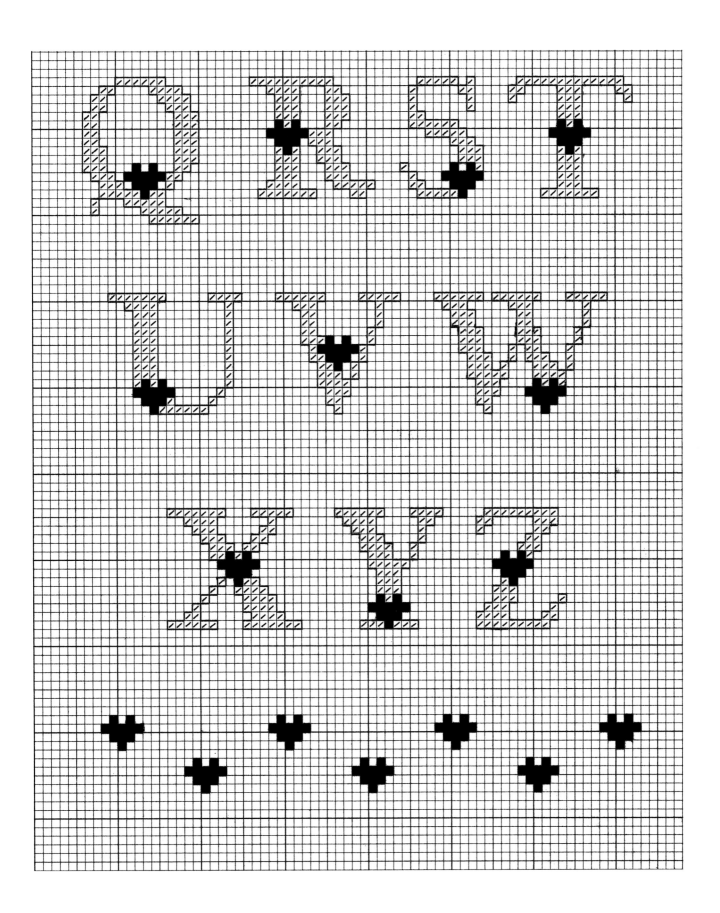

List of suppliers

UK

THREADS

Most needlecraft shops, haberdashery shops, large department stores and mail-order needlecraft suppliers stock either DMC or Anchor threads, sometimes both. Many of them also stock Coats and Madeira threads. For information on your nearest stockists, contact the customer-service departments of the firms themselves:

DMC
DMC Creative World Ltd
Pullman Road
Wigston
Leicester LE8 2DY

Anchor and Coats
Coats Leisure Crafts Group
39 Durham Street
Glasgow G41 1BS

Madeira
Madeira Threads (UK) Ltd
Thirsk Industrial Park
York Road
Thirsk
North Yorkshire YO7 3BX

GENERAL SUPPLIERS

It is a good idea to write to suppliers before sending money, just to check that they are still trading and that addresses are still valid.

Mary Allen
Wirksworth
Derbyshire DE4 4BN

Barnyarns
Old Pitts Farm
Langrish
Petersfield
Hampshire GU32 1RG

Campden Needlecraft Centre
High Street
Chipping Campden
Gloucestershire

Craft Basics
9 Gillygate
York YO3 7EA

John Lewis
Oxford Street
London W1

Needlecraft Needs
11 Leigh Road
Wimborne
Dorset BH21 1AB

Christine Riley
53 Barclay Street
Stonehaven
Kincardineshire AB3 2AR

Shades at Mace and Nairn
89 Crane Street
Salisbury
Wiltshire SP1 2PY

Silken Strands
33 Linksway
Gatley
Cheadle
Cheshire SK8 4LA

Threadbare
Glenfield Park
Glenfield Road
Nelson
Lancs BB9 8AR

Voirrey Embroidery
Brimstage Hall
Brimstage
Wirral L62 6JA

More suppliers can be found in *Embroidery*, a quarterly magazine published by the Embroiderers' Guild. Write to: Circulation Dept., PO Box 42B, East Molesey, Surrey KT8 9BB.

USA

American Thread Corporation
90 Park Avenue
New York

Appleton Brothers of London
West Main Road
Little Compton
Rhode Island 02837

Threadbenders
2260 Como Avenue
St Paul
Minnesota 55108

The Thread Connection
1020 East Carson Street
Pittsburgh
Pennsylvania 15203

The Thread Shed
307 Freeport Road
Pittsburgh
Pennsylvania 15215

WORLDWIDE

Framecraft Ltd is a mail-order company selling a wide variety of items for cross-stitch projects, including bookmarks, boxes, cards and accessories, frames, jewellery and kits.

ADDRESSES FOR FRAMECRAFT WORLDWIDE

Framecraft Miniatures Ltd
372–76 Summer Lane
Hockley
Birmingham B19 3QA
UK

Ireland Needlecraft Pty Ltd
2–4 Keppel Drive
Hallam
Victoria 3803
Australia

Danish Art Needlework
PO Box 442
Lethbridge
Alberta T1J 3Z1
Canada

Sanyei Imports
PO Box 5
Hashima Shi
Gifu 501–62
Japan

The Embroidery Shop
286 Queen Street
Masterton
New Zealand

S A Threads and Cottons Ltd
43 Somerset Road
Cape Town
South Africa

Anne Brinkley Designs Inc.
246 Walnut Street
Newton
Massachusetts 02160
USA